100 Turn-of-the-Century House Plans

The Radford Architectural Company

DOVER PUBLICATIONS, INC.
Mineola, New York

Copyright

All rights reserved under Pan American and International Copyright Conventions.

Published in Canada by General Publishing Company, Ltd., 30 Lesmill Road, Don Mills, Toronto, Ontario.

Bibliographical Note

This Dover edition, first published in 2000, is an unabridged republication of the 11th edition (1909) of the work published under the title *The Radford Ideal Homes: 100 House Plans* by The Radford Architectural Company, Chicago.

International Standard Book Number: 0-486-41251-2

Manufactured in the United States of America
Dover Publications, Inc., 31 East 2nd Street, Mineola, N.Y. 11501

The RADFORD Ideal Homes

100 House Plans 100

PRICE
$1.00

On the outside edge of each page where a house is illustrated, we publish the price at which full and complete working plans and specifications will be furnished. Please note the extremely low prices

PUBLISHED BY
THE RADFORD ARCHITECTURAL COMPANY
CHICAGO ::: RIVERSIDE
ILLINOIS, U. S. A.

Original title page

THE RADFORD IDEAL HOMES

ELEVENTH EDITION :: :: :: :: FEBRUARY, 1903

IN PRESENTING this, the eleventh edition of THE RADFORD IDEAL HOMES to the public, the publishers wish to thank those who have shown so much appreciation for the first ten editions, and who have shown their appreciation not only by ordering the books, but by buying and favorably commenting on the blue prints and specifications. The encouragement we have received has been the means of urging us to print this tenth issue in larger quantity than heretofore. As the houses are moderate in price and convenient in arrangement, we feel sure of securing liberal patronage. In the planning of all our designs, we have recognized the fact that the people of to-day demand modern appearances, as well as the different conveniences, when they decide upon building a home. A great deal of time and study has been spent on each design, and every set of plans will be found complete and accurate in all details, no labor having been spared where any small advantage could be gained. Many people are surprised that we can furnish blue prints and specifications of such up-to-date houses at the price for which we advertise them, and we could not were it not for the fact that we have succeeded in supplying the demand for the very thing that the people have been looking for, namely, a moderate priced, convenient house. All of these plans have been made for us by a licensed architect of the State of Illinois. They are accurate and complete in every detail.

WHAT WE FURNISH IN BLUE PRINTS

Foundation and Cellar Plan This sheet shows the shape and size of all walls, piers, footings, posts, etc., and of what materials they are constructed; shows the location of all windows, doors, chimneys, ash-pits, partitions and the like. The different wall sections are given, showing their construction, and measurements are given from all the different points.

Floor Plans These plans show the shape and size of all rooms, halls and closets, the location and sizes of all doors and windows, the position of all plumbing fixtures, gas lights, registers, pantry work, etc. All measurements that are necessary are given.

Elevations A front, right, left and rear elevations are furnished with all plans. These drawings are complete and accurate in every respect. They show the shape, size and location of all doors and windows, porches, cornices, towers, bays, and the like, and in fact give you an exact scale picture of the house as it should be at completion. Full wall sections are given, showing the construction from foundation to roof, the height of stories between joists, height of plates, pitch of roofs, etc.

Roof Plan This plan is furnished where the roof construction is at all intricate. It shows the location of all hips, valleys, ridges, decks, etc. All the above drawings are made a quarter of an inch to the foot.

Details All necessary details of the interior work, such as door and window casings, and trim, base, stools, picture moulding, doors, newelposts, balusters, rails, etc., accompany each set of plans; part is shown in full size, while some of the larger work, such as stair construction, is drawn to a scale of inch and a half to the foot.

Lumber Bill We do not furnish a lumber bill. We state this here, as some people seem to think that a lumber bill should accompany each set of specifications. In the first place, our plans are gotten up very plain, and any carpenter who cannot in a few minutes take off the bill of lumber from these plans is not the man to build your house. Another reason why we send no lumber bill is that houses from these designs are being built in all parts of the country; from the Atlantic to the Pacific and from Hudson Bay to the Gulf of Mexico. Houses when finished may look the same, whether built in Florida or Canada, but the same material would not be used, for the reason that custom and the seasons will it differently.

Change of Plans We cannot change our plans for the reason that every plan we have drawn is used as a negative, and the blue prints we sell you are photographed from that negative.

THE RADFORD ARCHITECTURAL COMPANY, Publishers
CHICAGO :: RIVERSIDE
ILLINOIS, U. S. A.

PRICE of Blue Prints, together with a complete set of typewritten specifications, is

$5.00

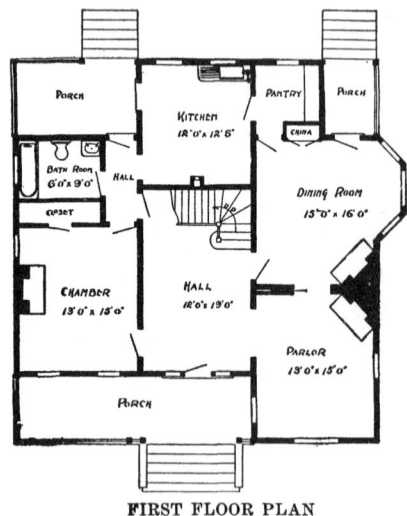

FIRST FLOOR PLAN

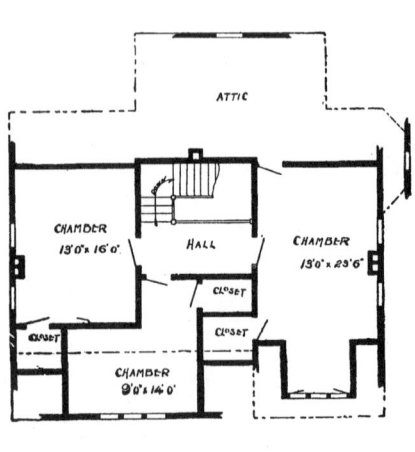

SECOND FLOOR PLAN

Design No. 86
Cost about $1,500

Size: width, 40 feet; length, 40 feet. Blue prints consist of foundation plan; floor plan; front, rear, two side elevations; wall sections and all necessary interior details.

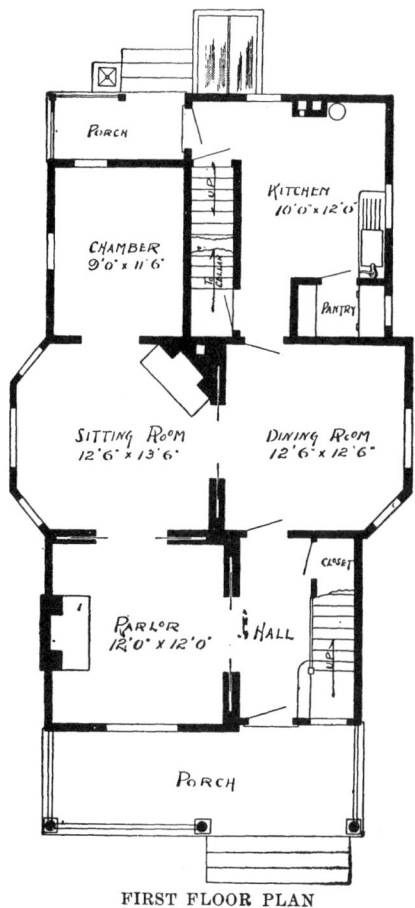

FIRST FLOOR PLAN

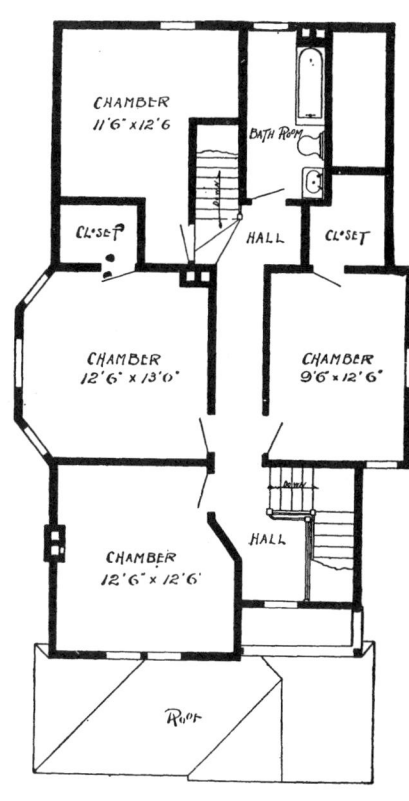

SECOND FLOOR PLAN

PRICE of Blue Prints, together with a complete set of typewritten specifications, is

$5.00

Size: width, 28 feet; length, 45 feet exclusive of porch. Blue prints consist of cellar and foundation plan; first and second floor plans; front, rear, two side elevations; wall sections and all necessary interior details.

Design No. 82
Cost about $2,000

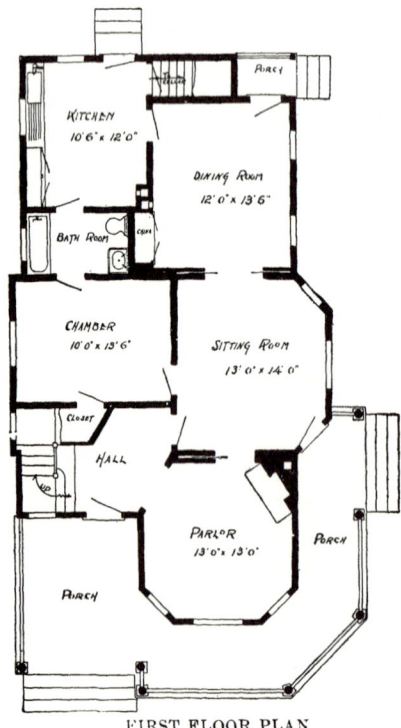

FIRST FLOOR PLAN

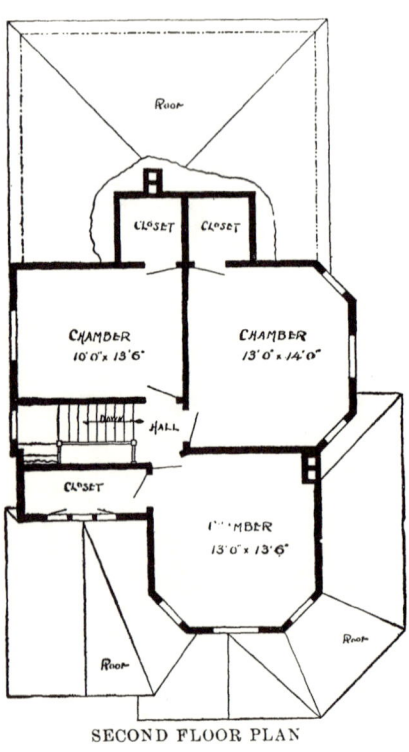

SECOND FLOOR PLAN

PRICE of Blue Prints, together with a complete set of typewritten specifications, is

$5.00

Design No. 84
Cost about $1,900

Size: width, 28 feet; length, 47 feet exclusive of porches. Blue prints consist of cellar and foundation plan; first and second floor plans; front, rear, two side elevations; wall sections and all necessary interior details.

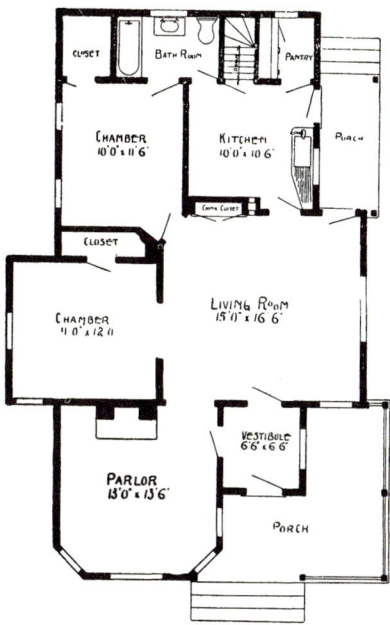

FLOOR PLAN

PRICE of Blue Prints, together with a complete set of typewritten specifications, is

$5.00

Size: width, 30 feet; length, 46 feet exclusive of porches. Blue prints consist of cellar and foundation plan; floor and roof plans; front, rear, two side elevations; wall sections and all necessary interior details.

Design No. 45
Cost about $1,300

PRICE of Blue Prints, together with a complete set of typewritten specifications, is

$5.00

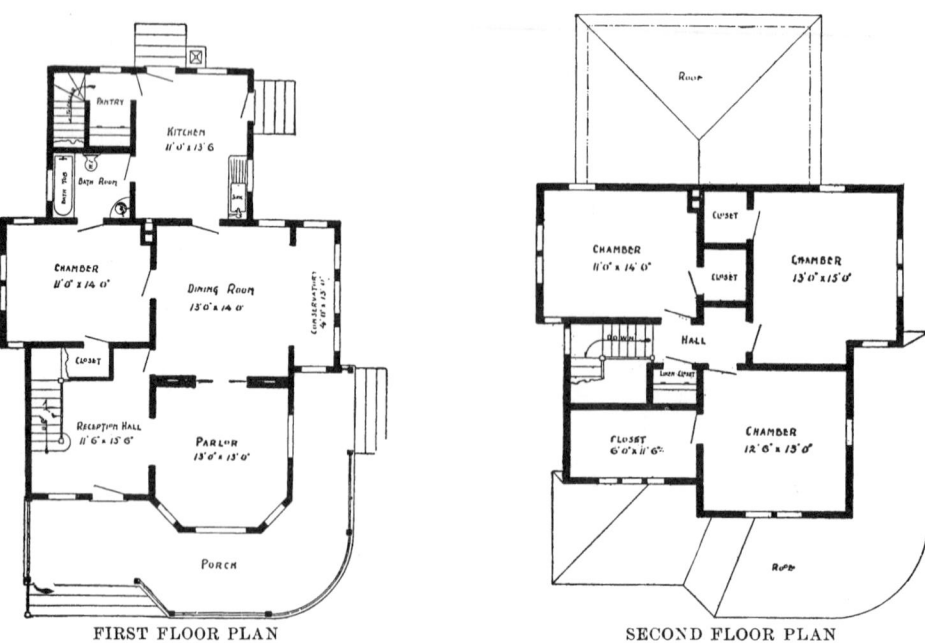

FIRST FLOOR PLAN   SECOND FLOOR PLAN

Design No. 71
Cost about $1,500

Size: width, 33 feet; length, 43 feet exclusive of porch. Blue prints consist of cellar and foundation plan; first and second floor plans; front, rear, two side elevations; wall sections and all necessary interior details.

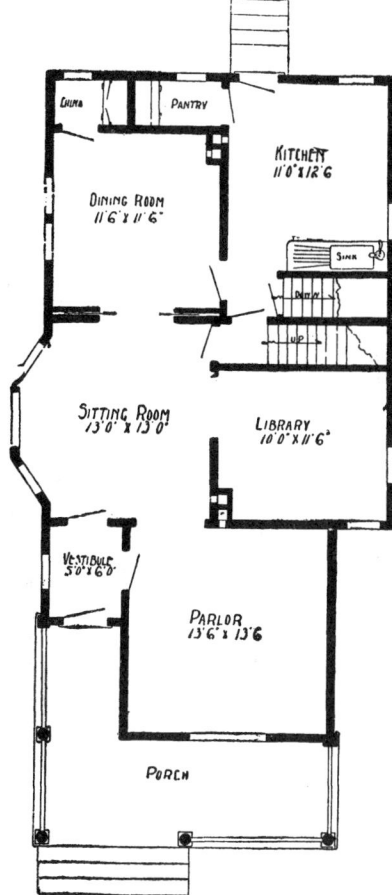

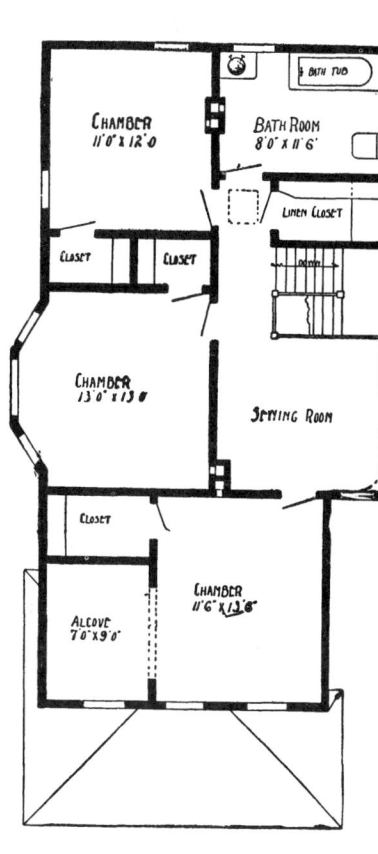

FIRST FLOOR PLAN — SECOND FLOOR PLAN

PRICE of Blue Prints, together with a complete set of typewritten specifications, is

$5.00

Size: width, 26 feet; length, 44 feet exclusive of porch. Blue prints consist of cellar and foundation plan; first and second floor plans; front, rear, two side elevations; wall sections and all necessary interior details.

Design No. 43
Cost about $1,750

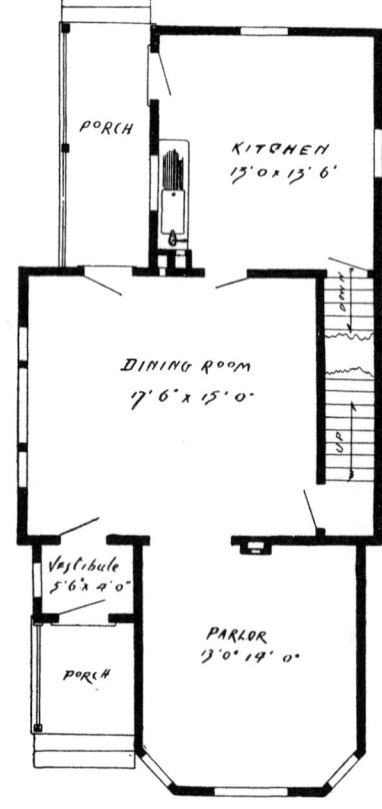

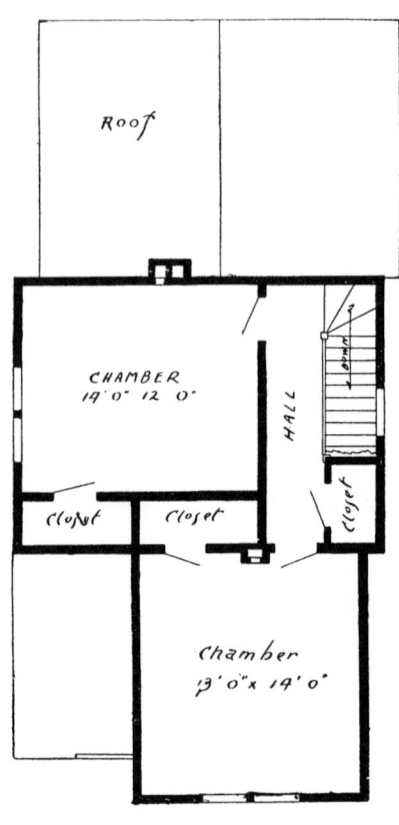

PRICE of Blue Prints, together with a complete set of typewritten specifications, is

$3.00

FIRST FLOOR PLAN

SECOND FLOOR PLAN

Design No. 20
Cost about $850

Size: width, 22 feet; length, 44 feet. Blue prints consist of cellar and foundation plan; first and second floor plans; front, rear, two side elevations; wall sections and all necessary interior details

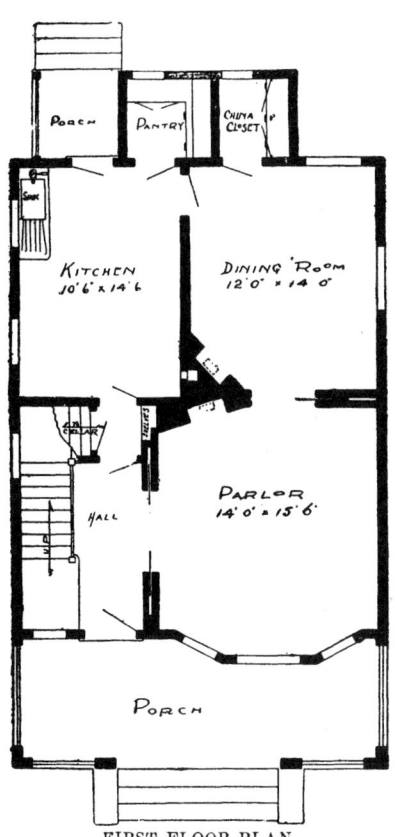

FIRST FLOOR PLAN

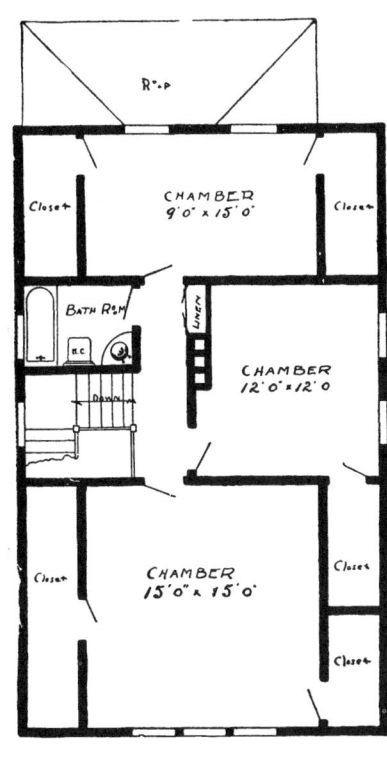

SECOND FLOOR PLAN

PRICE of Blue Prints, together with a complete set of typewritten specifications, is

$5.00

Size: width, 24 feet; length, 38 feet. Blue prints consist of cellar and foundation plan; first and second floor plans; front, rear, two side elevations; wall sections and all necessary interior details.

Design No. 37
Cost about $1,500

PRICE of Blue Prints, together with a complete set of typewritten specifications, is

$5.00

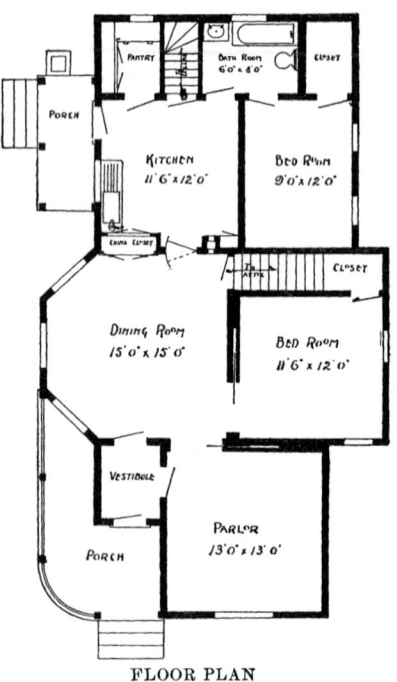

FLOOR PLAN

Design No. 78
Cost about $1,000

Size: width, 29 feet; length, 49 feet. Blue prints consist of cellar and foundation plan; floor plan; front, rear, two side elevations; wall sections and all necessary interior details.

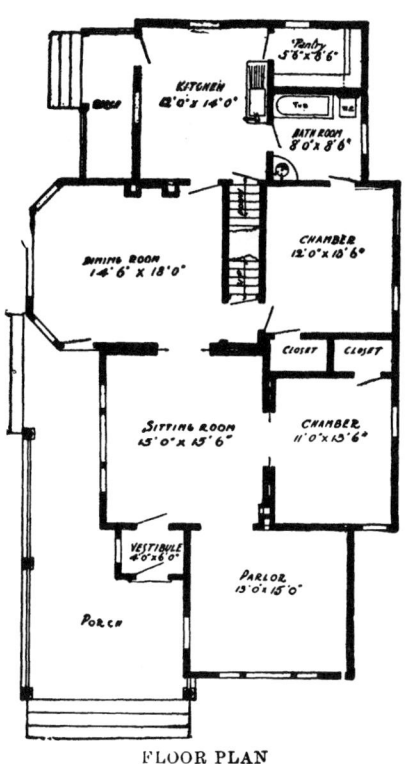

FLOOR PLAN

PRICE of Blue Prints, together with a complete set of typewritten specifications, is

$5.00

Size: width, 34 feet; length, 60 feet. Blue prints consist of cellar and foundation plan; floor plan; roof plan, front, rear, two side elevations; wall sections and all necessary interior details.

Design No. 17
Cost about $1,400

PRICE of Blue Prints, together with a complete set of typewritten specifications, is

$3.00

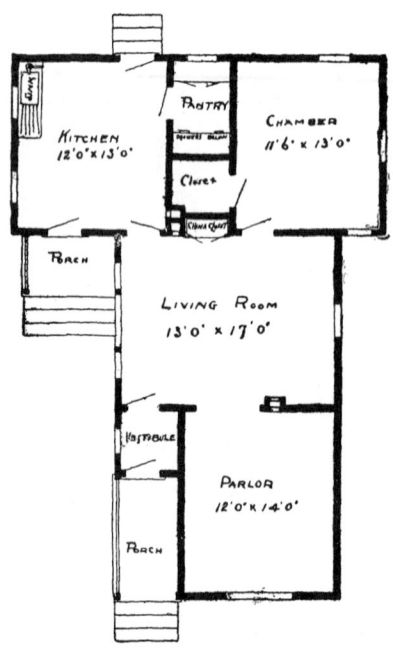

FLOOR PLAN

Design No. 24
Cost about $900

Size: width, 30 feet; length, 42 feet. Blue prints consist of foundation plan; floor plan; front, rear, two side elevations; wall sections and all necessary interior details.

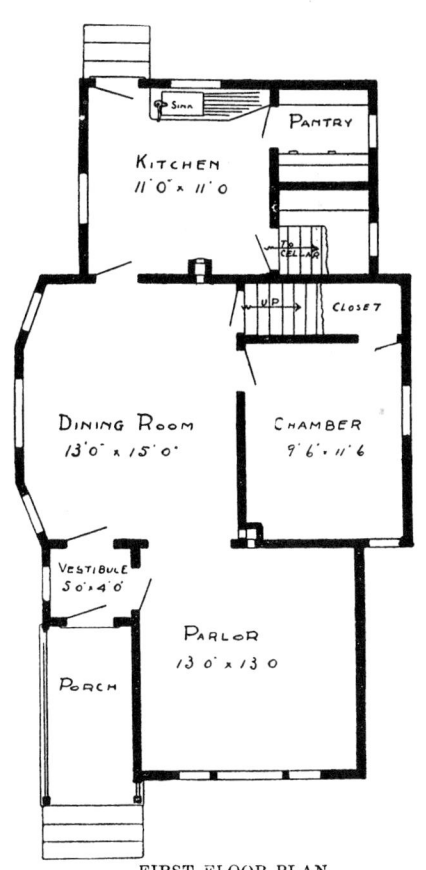

FIRST FLOOR PLAN

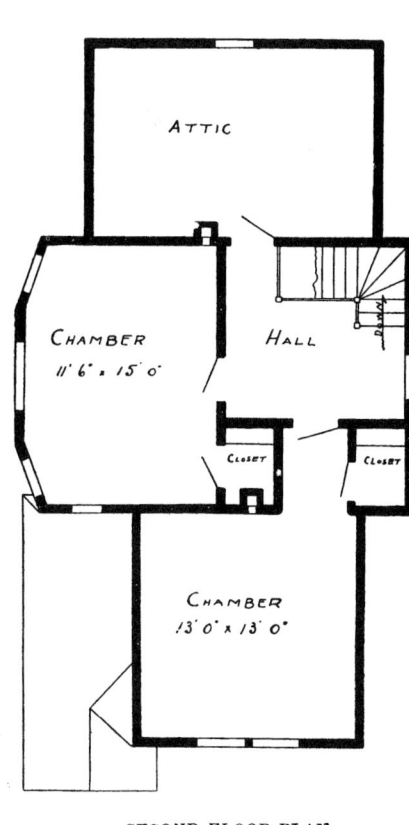

SECOND FLOOR PLAN

PRICE of Blue Prints, together with a complete set of typewritten specifications, is

$4.00

Size: width, 24 feet; length, 41 feet. Blue prints consist of cellar and foundation plan; first and second floor plans; front, rear, two side elevations; wall sections and all necessary interior details.

Design No. 34
Cost about $1,100

15

P R I C E
of Blue Prints,
together with a
complete set of
typewritten
specifications, is

$3.00

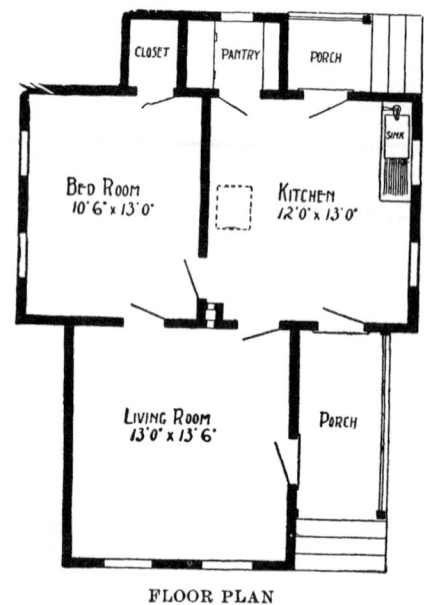

FLOOR PLAN

Design No. 42
Cost about $500

Size: width, 24 feet; length, 32 feet. Blue prints consist of foundation plan; floor plan; front, rear, two side elevations; wall sections and all necessary interior details

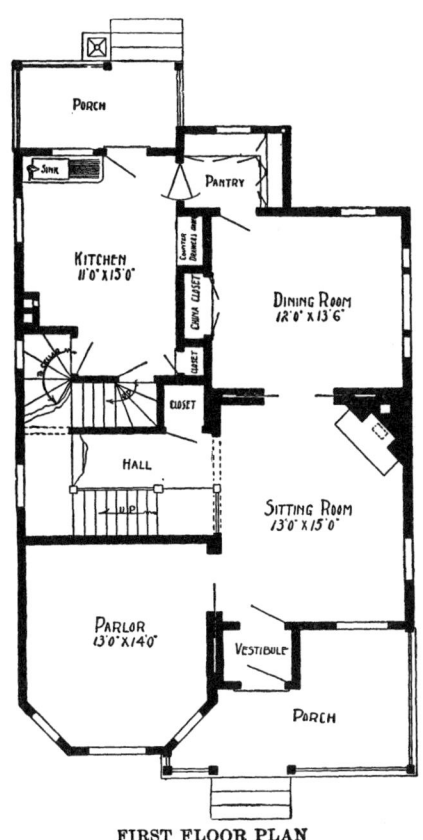

FIRST FLOOR PLAN

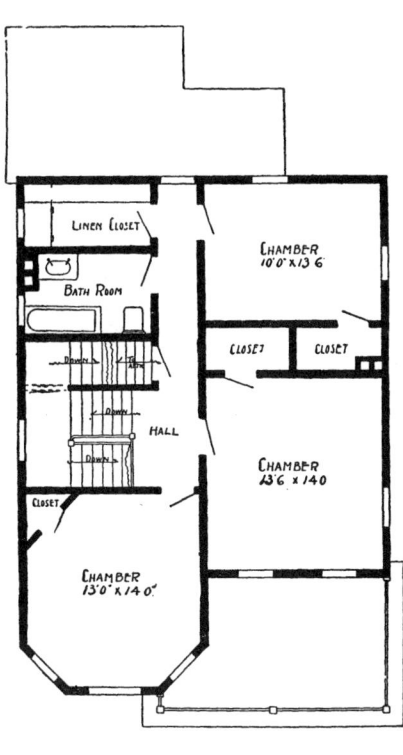

SECOND FLOOR PLAN

PRICE of Blue Prints, together with a complete set of typewritten specifications, is

$5.00

Size: width, 28 feet; length, 42 feet exclusive of porches. Blue prints consist of cellar and foundation plan; first and second floor plans; roof plan; front, rear, two side elevations; wall sections and all necessary interior details.

Design No. 41
Cost about $2,250

17

PRICE of Blue Prints, together with a complete set of typewritten specifications, is

$5.00

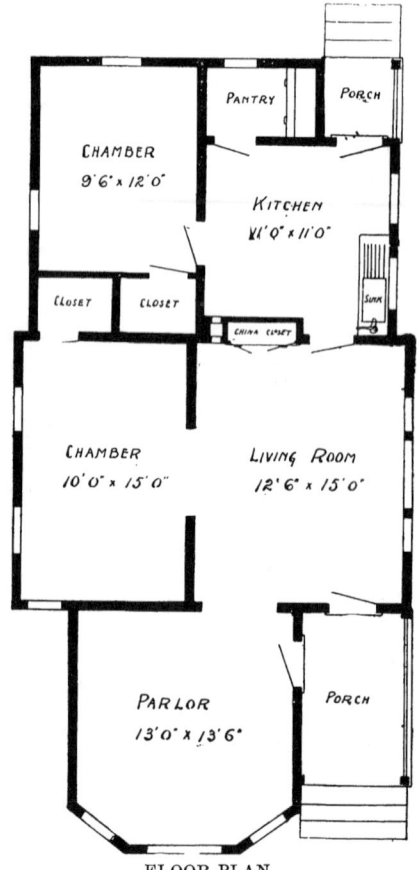

FLOOR PLAN

Design No. 76
Cost about $850

Size: width, 24 feet; length, 46 feet. Blue prints consist of foundation plan; floor plans; front, rear, two side elevations; wall sections and all necessary interior details.

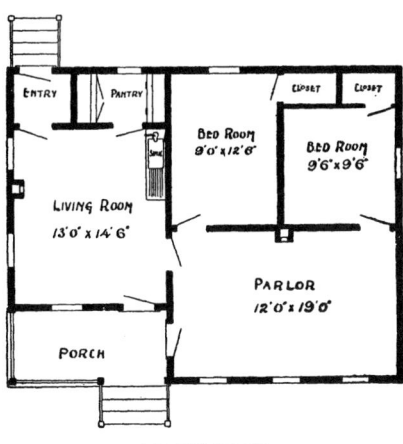

FLOOR PLAN

PRICE of Blue Prints, together with a complete set of typewritten specifications, is

$5.00

Size: width, 33 feet, 6 inches; length, 26 feet. Blue prints consist of foundation plan; floor plan; front, rear, two side elevations; wall sections and all necessary interior details.

Design No. 69
Cost about $600

PRICE of Blue Prints, together with a complete set of typewritten specifications, is

$4.00

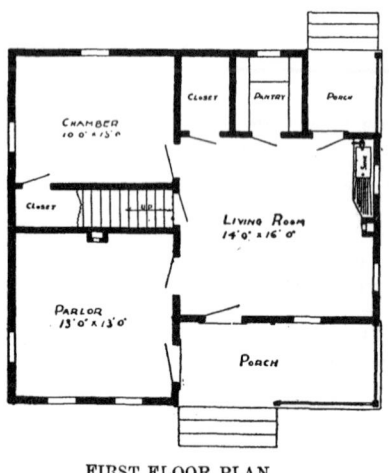

FIRST FLOOR PLAN

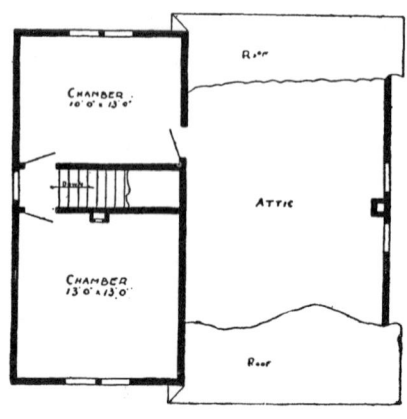

SECOND FLOOR PLAN

Design No. 39
Cost about $900

Size: width, 30 feet; length, 28 feet. Blue prints consist of foundation plan; first and second floor plans; front, rear, two side elevations; wall sections and all necessary interior details.

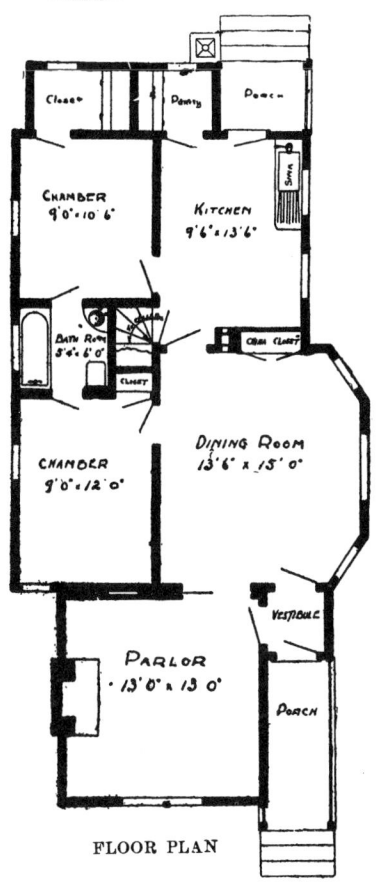

FLOOR PLAN

PRICE of Blue Prints, together with a complete set of typewritten specifications, is

$4.00

Size: width, 24 feet; length, 48 feet exclusive of porches. Blue prints consist of cellar and foundation plan; floor plan; front, rear, two side elevations; wall sections and all necessary interior details.

Design No. 38
Cost about $1,000

21

PRICE of Blue Prints, together with a complete set of typewritten specifications, is

$8.00

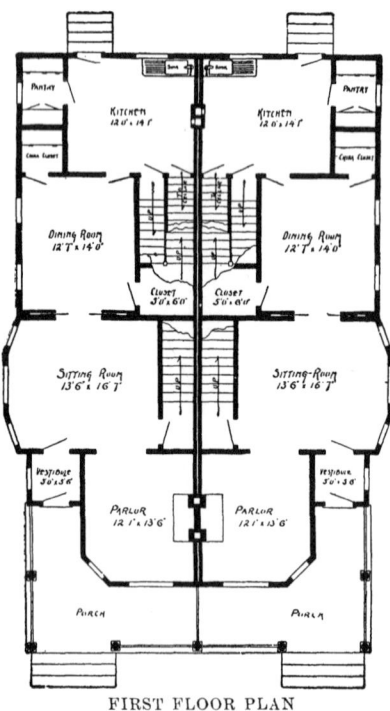

FIRST FLOOR PLAN

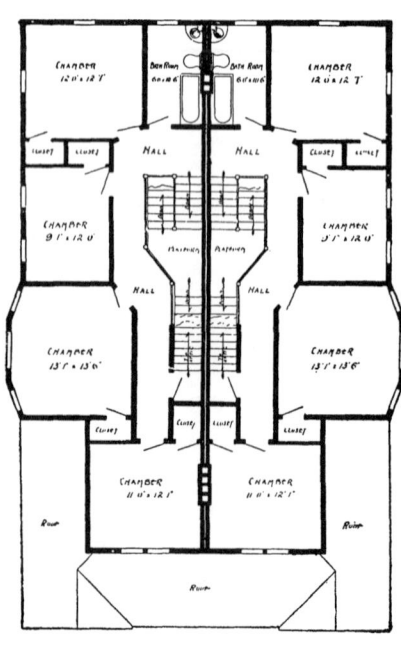

SECOND FLOOR PLAN

Design No. 56
Cost about $4,000

Size: width, 43 feet; length, 56 feet exclusive of porch. Blue prints consist of cellar and foundation plan; first and second floor plans; front, rear, two side elevations; wall sections and all necessary interior details.

PRICE of Blue Prints, together with a complete set of typewritten specifications, is

$12.00

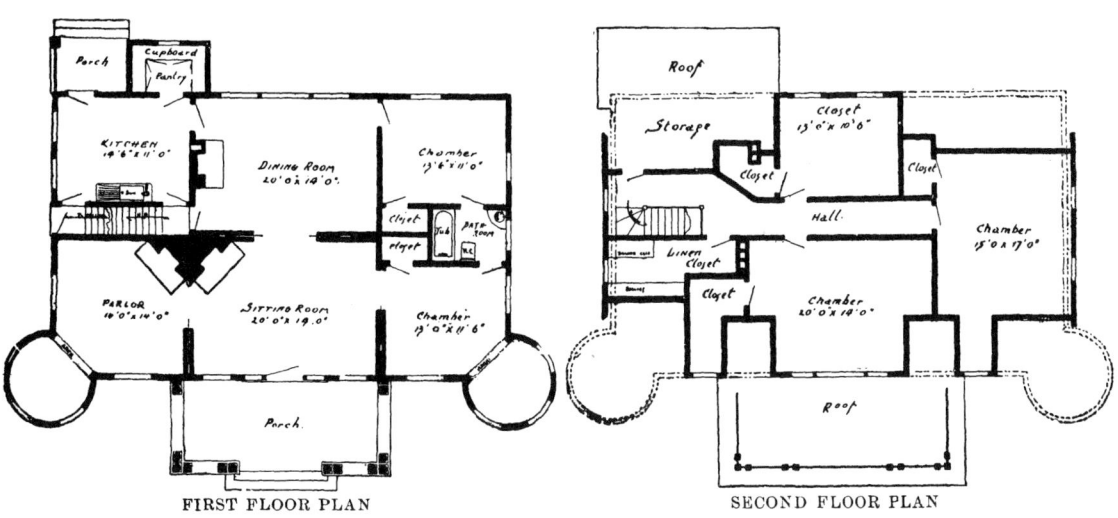

FIRST FLOOR PLAN   SECOND FLOOR PLAN

Size: width, 50 feet; length, 30 feet exclusive of porches. Blue prints consist of cellar and foundation plan; first and second floor plans; roof plan; front, rear, two side elevations; wall sections and all necessary interior details.

Design No. 22
Cost about $3,500

PRICE of Blue Prints, together with a complete set of typewritten specifications, is

$3.00

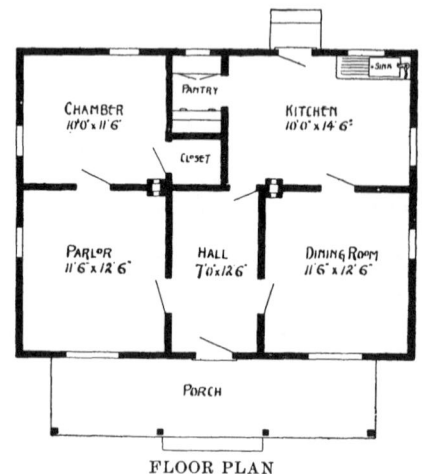

FLOOR PLAN

Design No. 48
Cost about $600

Size: width, 32 feet; length, 24 feet exclusive of porch. Blue prints consist of foundation plan; floor plan; front, rear, two side elevations; wall sections and all necessary interior details.

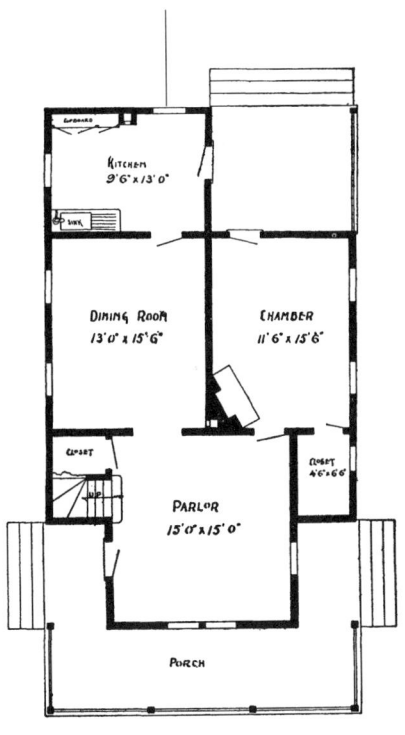

FIRST FLOOR PLAN

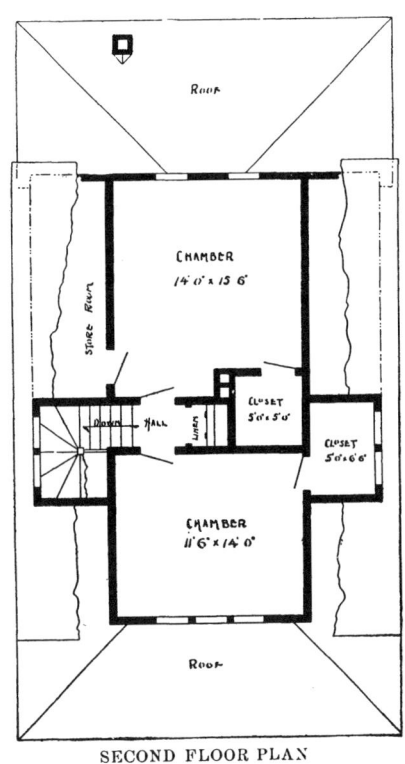

SECOND FLOOR PLAN

PRICE of Blue Prints, together with a complete set of typewritten specifications, is

$5.00

Size: width, 26 feet; length, 42 feet exclusive of porch. Blue prints consist of foundation plan; first and second floor plans; front, rear, two side elevations; wall sections and all necessary interior details.

Design No. 72
Cost about $900

PRICE of Blue Prints, together with a complete set of typewritten specifications, is

$5.00

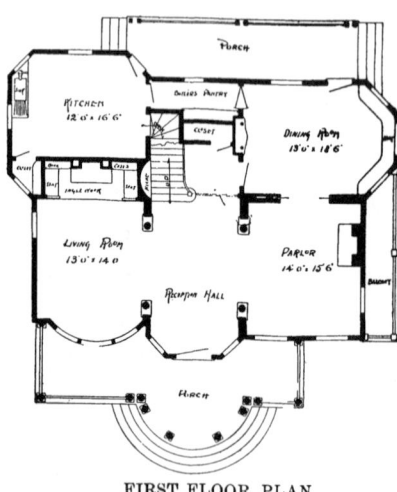

FIRST FLOOR PLAN

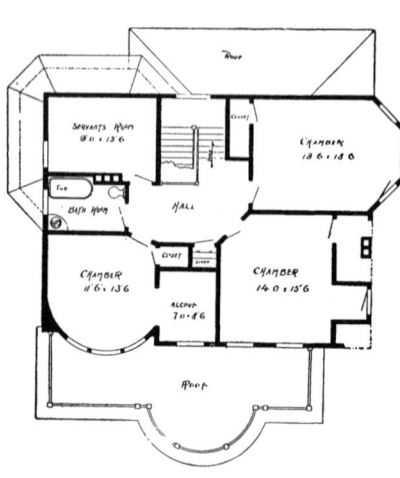

SECOND FLOOR PLAN

Design No. 91
Cost about $3,000

Size: width, 48 feet; length, 36 feet exclusive of porches. Blue prints consist of cellar and foundation plan; first and second floor plans; front, rear, two side elevations; wall sections, all necessary interior details.

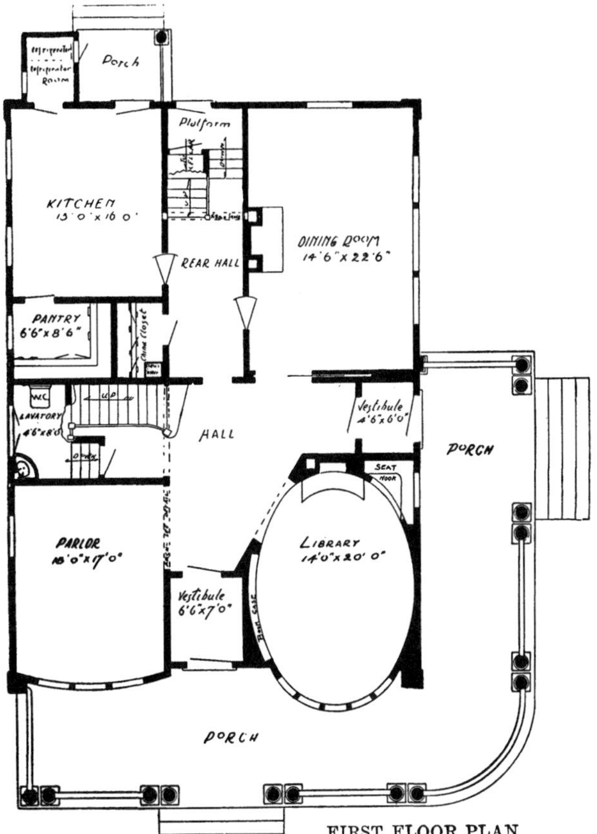

Size: width, 36 feet; length, 50 feet exclusive of porches. Blue prints consist of cellar and foundation plan; first and second floor plans; front, rear, two side elevations; wall sections, all necessary interior and exterior details

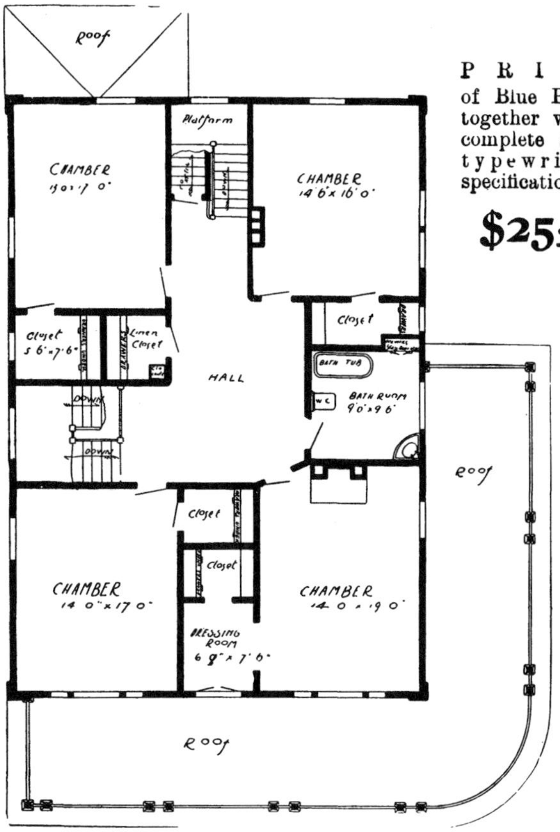

Design No. 7
Cost about $6,500

PRICE of Blue Prints, together with a complete set of typewritten specifications, is

$3.00

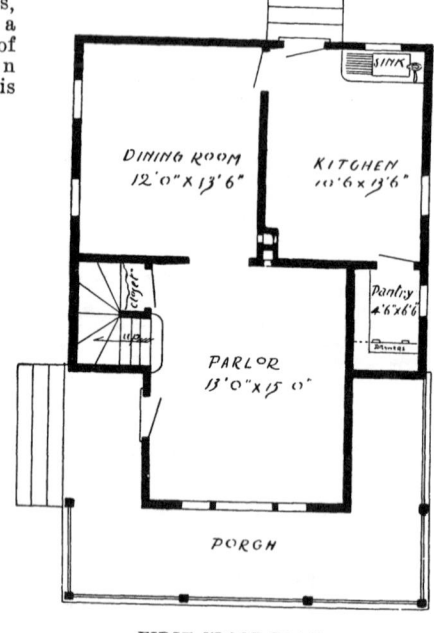

FIRST FLOOR PLAN

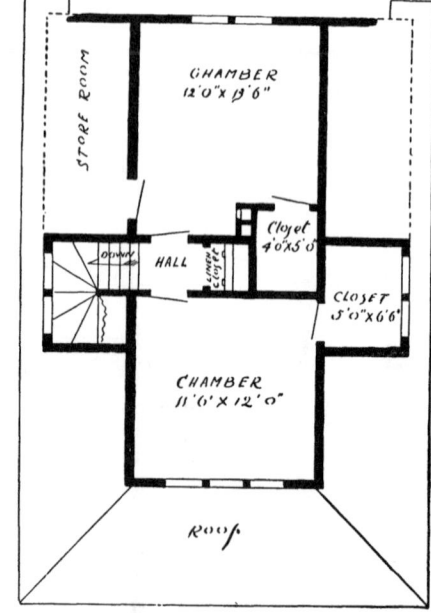

SECOND FLOOR PLAN

Design No. 2
Cost about $800

Size: width, 24 feet; length, 30 feet exclusive of porch. Blue prints consist of cellar and foundation plan; first and second floor plans; front, rear, two side elevations; wall sections and all necessary interior details.

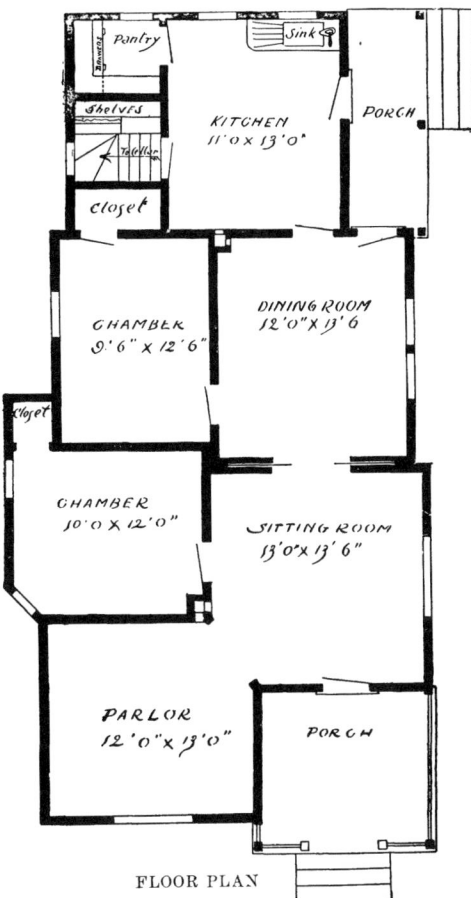

FLOOR PLAN

PRICE of Blue Prints, together with a complete set of typewritten specifications, is

$4.00

Size: width, 27 feet; length, 50 feet exclusive of porches. Blue prints consist of cellar and foundation plan; floor plan; roof plan; front, rear, two side elevations; wall sections and all necessary interior details.

Design No. 1
Cost about $1,200

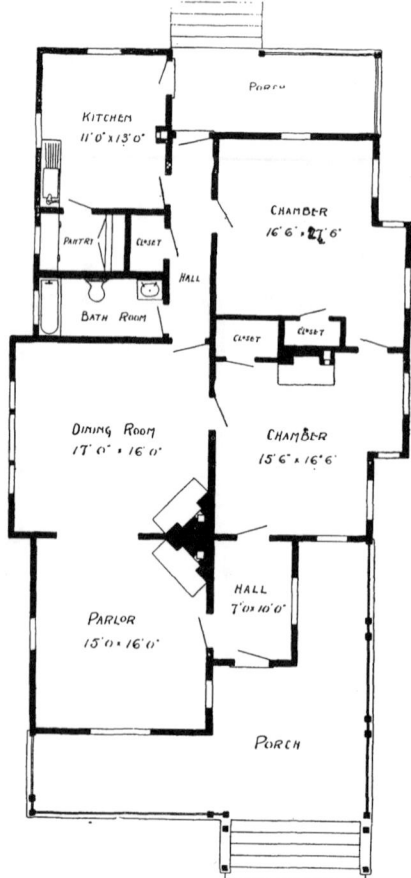

FLOOR PLAN

PRICE of Blue Prints, together with a complete set of typewritten specifications, is

$5.00

Design No. 75
Cost about $1,400

Size: width, 35 feet; length, 59 feet exclusive of porch. Blue prints consist of foundation plan; floor plan; front, rear, two side elevations; wall sections and all necessary interior details.

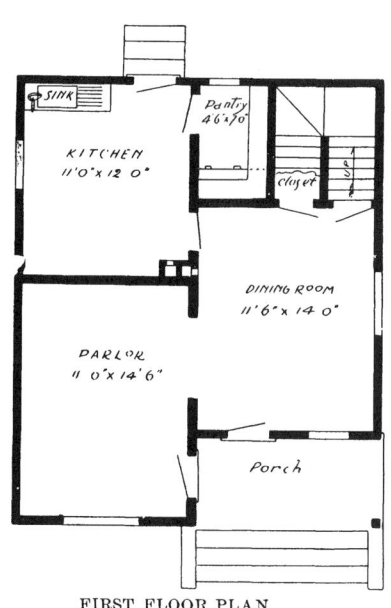

FIRST FLOOR PLAN

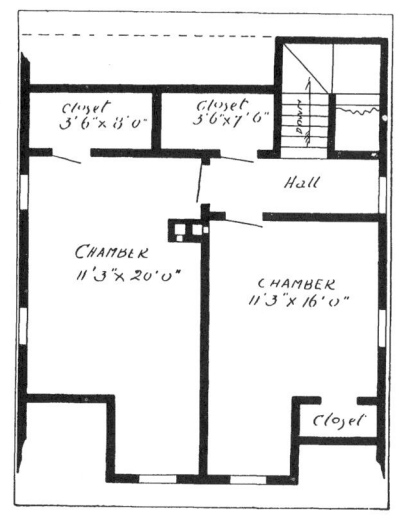

SECOND FLOOR PLAN

PRICE of Blue Prints, together with a complete set of typewritten specifications, is

$3.00

Size: width, 24 feet; length, 28 feet. Blue prints consist of foundation plan; first and second floor plans; front, rear, two side elevations; wall sections and all necessary interior details.

Design No. 5
Cost about $700

31

PRICE of Blue Prints, together with a complete set of typewritten specifications, is

$4.00

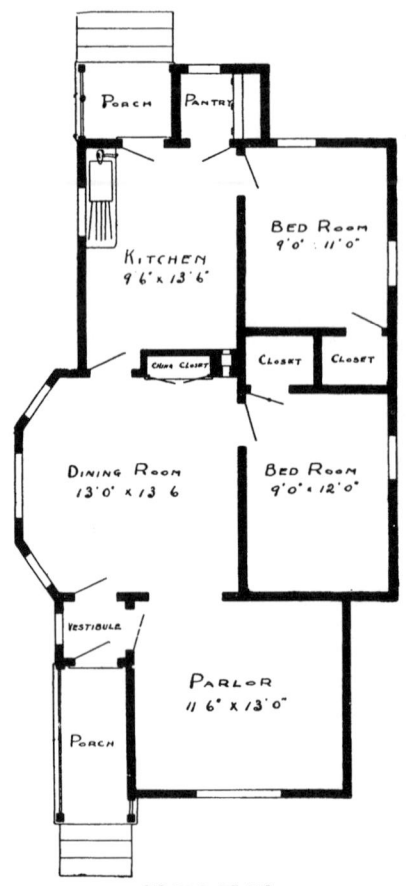

FLOOR PLAN

Design No. 35
Cost about $900

Size: width, 24 feet; length, 40 feet. Blue prints consist of foundation plan; floor plan; front, rear, two side elevations; wall sections and all necessary interior details.

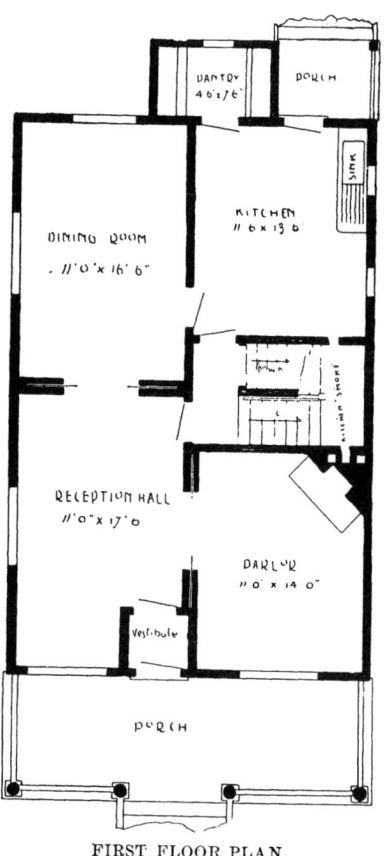

FIRST FLOOR PLAN

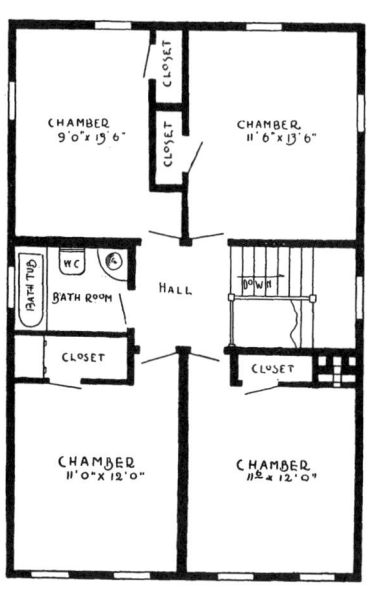

SECOND FLOOR PLAN

PRICE of Blue Prints, together with a complete set of typewritten specifications, is

$4.00

Size: width, 24 feet; length, 36 feet exclusive of porches. Blue prints consist of cellar and foundation plan; first and second floor plans; roof plan; front, rear, two side elevations; wall sections and all necessary interior details.

Design No. 6
Cost about $1,800

PRICE of Blue prints, together with a complete set of typewritten specifications, is

$4.00

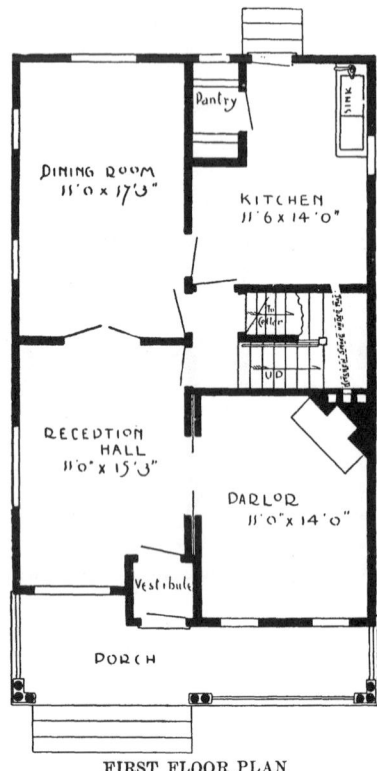

FIRST FLOOR PLAN

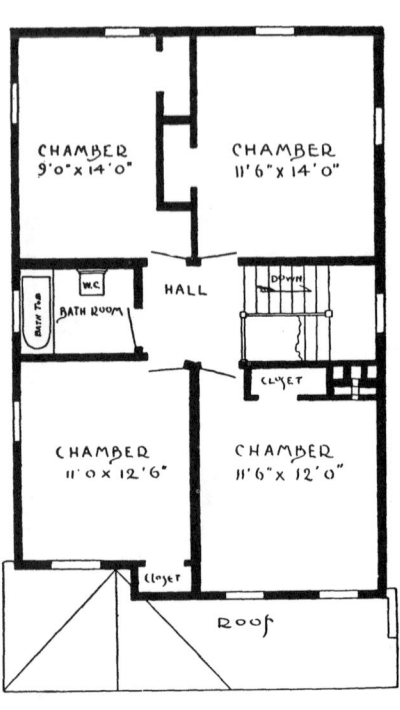

SECOND FLOOR PLAN

Design No. 10
Cost about $1,500

Size: width, 24 feet; length, 36 feet exclusive of porch. Blue prints consist of cellar and foundation plan; first and second floor plans; front, rear, two side elevations; wall sections and all necessary interior details.

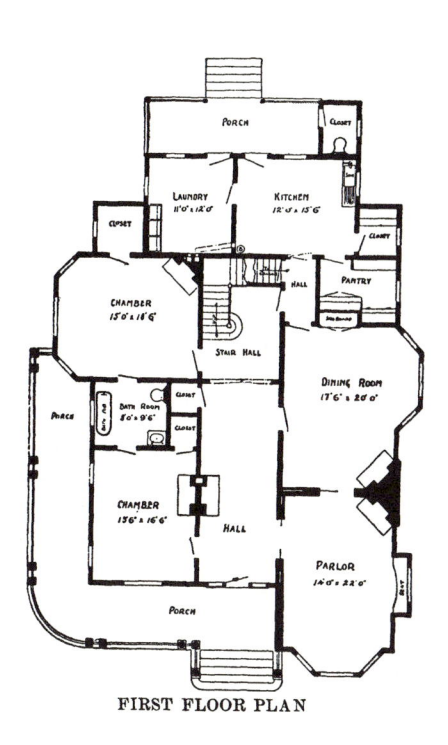

FIRST FLOOR PLAN

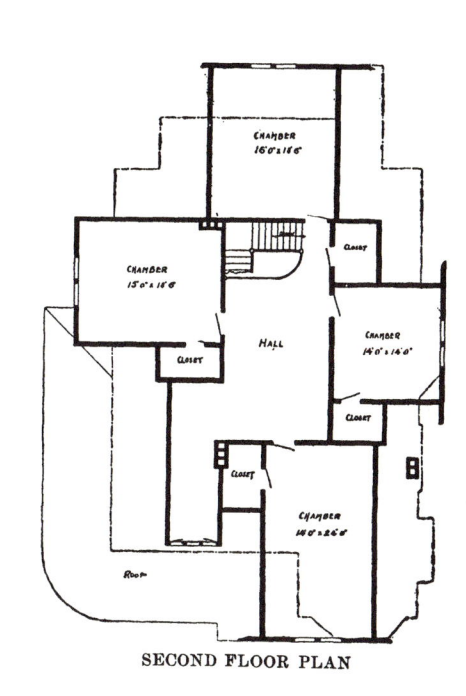

SECOND FLOOR PLAN

PRICE of Blue Prints, together with a complete set of typewritten specifications, is

$8.00

Size: width, 46 feet; length, 64 feet exclusive of porches. Blue prints consist of cellar and foundation plan; first and second floor plans; front, rear, two side elevations; wall sections and all necessary interior details.

Design No. 73
Cost about $2,800

35

PRICE of Blue Prints, together with a complete set of typewritten specifications, is

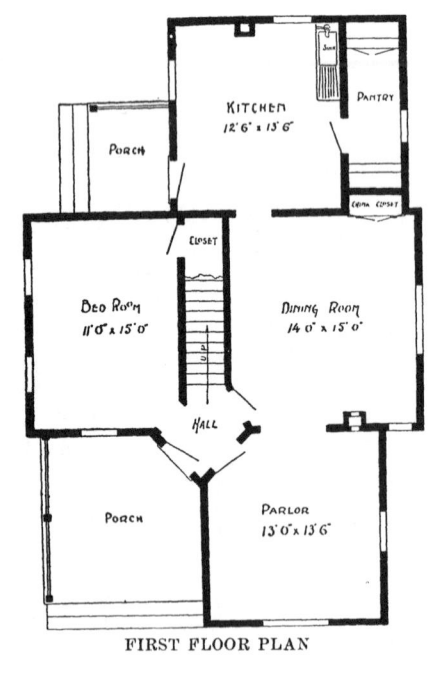

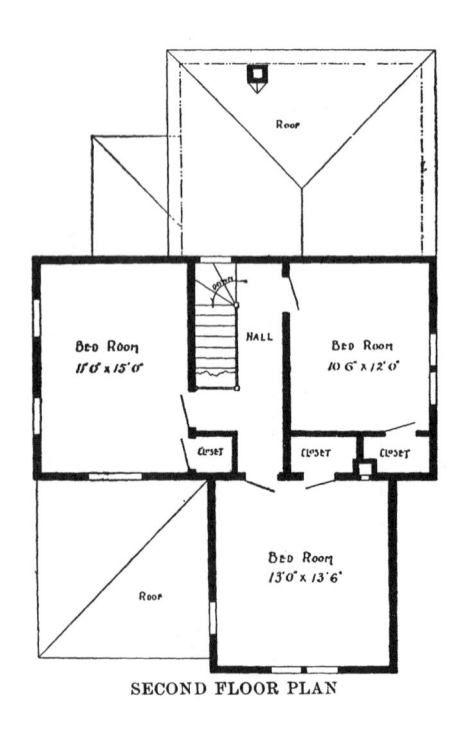

$5.00

FIRST FLOOR PLAN

SECOND FLOOR PLAN

Design No. 74
Cost about $1,000

Size: width, 30 feet; length, 44 feet. Blue prints consist of foundation plan; first and second floor plans; front, rear, two side elevations; wall sections and all necessary interior details.

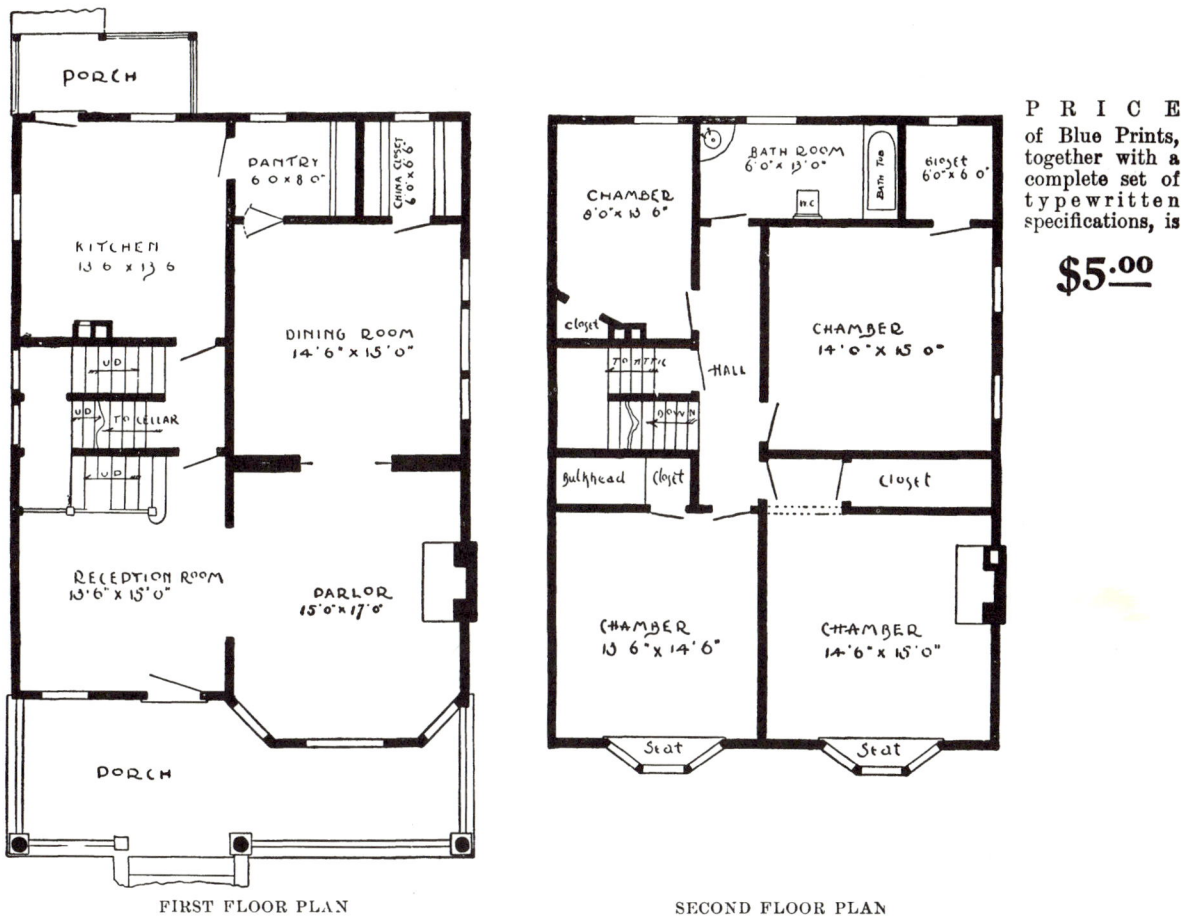

FIRST FLOOR PLAN

SECOND FLOOR PLAN

PRICE of Blue Prints, together with a complete set of typewritten specifications, is

$5.⁰⁰

Size: width, 30 feet; length, 40 feet exclusive of porches. Blue prints consist of cellar and foundation plan; first and second floor plans; roof and attic plan; front, rear, two side elevations; wall sections and all necessary interior details.

Design No. 9
Cost about $2,500

PRICE
of Blue Prints,
together with a
complete set of
typewritten
specifications, is

$5.00

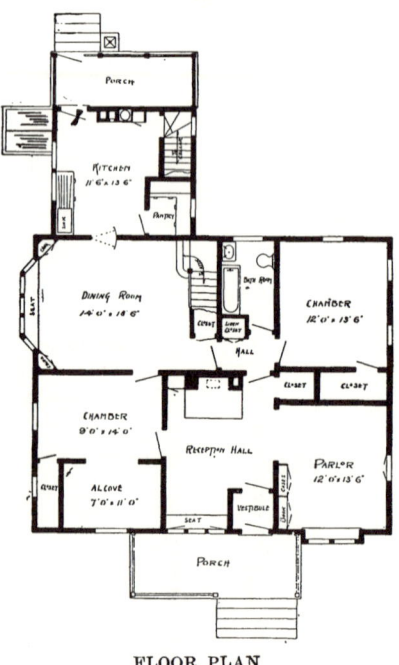

FLOOR PLAN

Design No. 81
Cost about $2,000

Size: width, 40 feet; length, 44 feet exclusive of porches. Blue prints consist of cellar and foundation plan; floor plan; front, rear, two side elevations; wall sections and all necessary interior details.

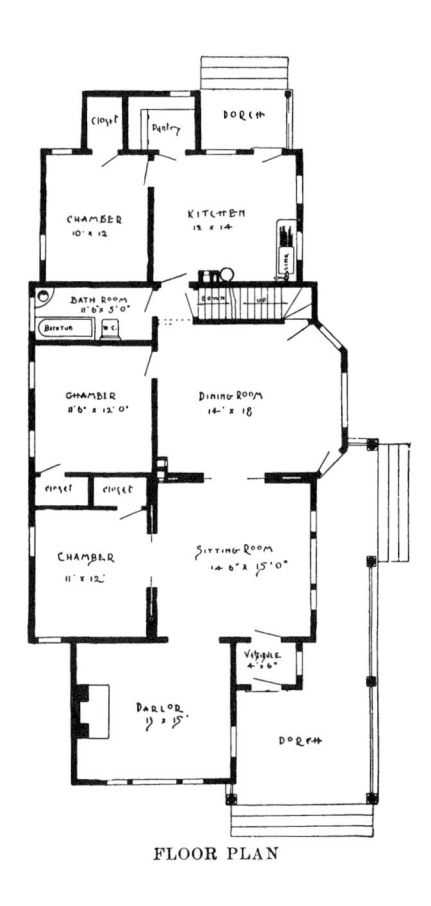

FLOOR PLAN

PRICE of Blue Prints, together with a complete set of typewritten specifications, is

$5.00

Size: width, 31 feet; length, 60 feet exclusive of porches. Blue prints consist of cellar and foundation plan; floor plan; front, rear, two side elevations; wall sections and all necessary interior details.

Design No. 16
Cost about $1,500

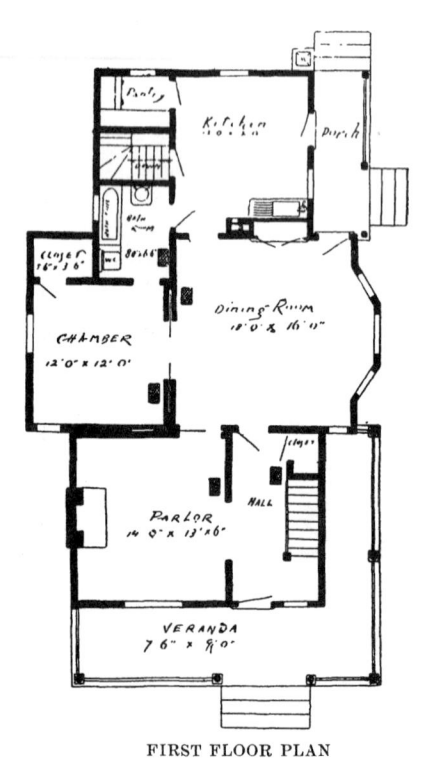

FIRST FLOOR PLAN   SECOND FLOOR PLAN

PRICE of Blue Prints, together with a complete set of typewritten specifications, is

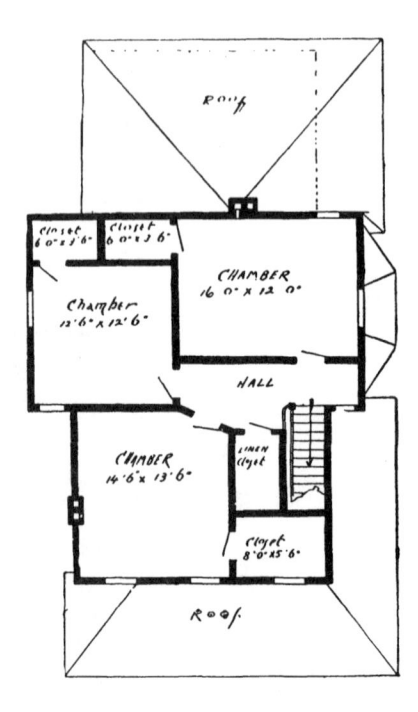

$4.50

Design No. 14
Cost about $1,500

Size: width, 32 feet; length, 46 feet exclusive of porches. Blue prints consist of cellar and foundation plan; first and second floor plans; front, rear, two side elevations; wall sections and all necessary interior details.

40

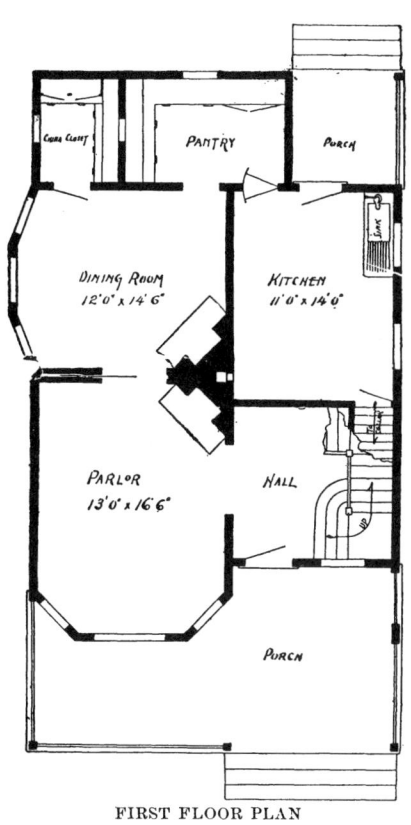

FIRST FLOOR PLAN

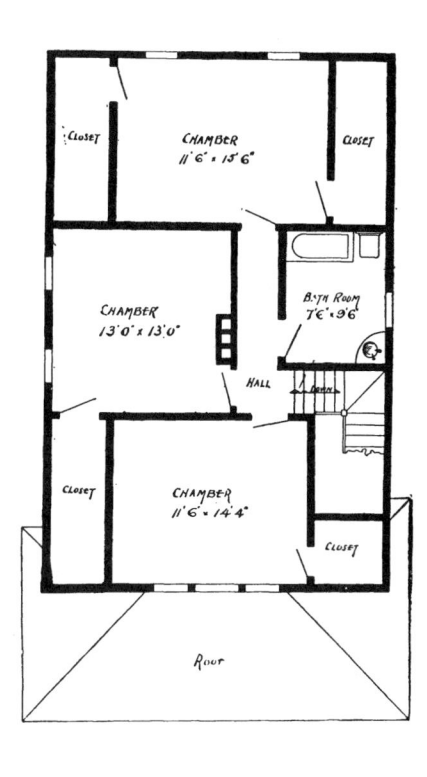

SECOND FLOOR PLAN

PRICE of Blue Prints, together with a complete set of typewritten specifications, is

$5.00

Size: width, 27 feet; length, 38 feet exclusive of porches. Blue prints consist of cellar and foundation plan; first and second floor plans; front, **rear,** two side elevations; wall sections and all necessary interior details.

Design No. 57
Cost about $1,500

PRICE of Blue Prints, together with a complete set of typewritten specifications, is

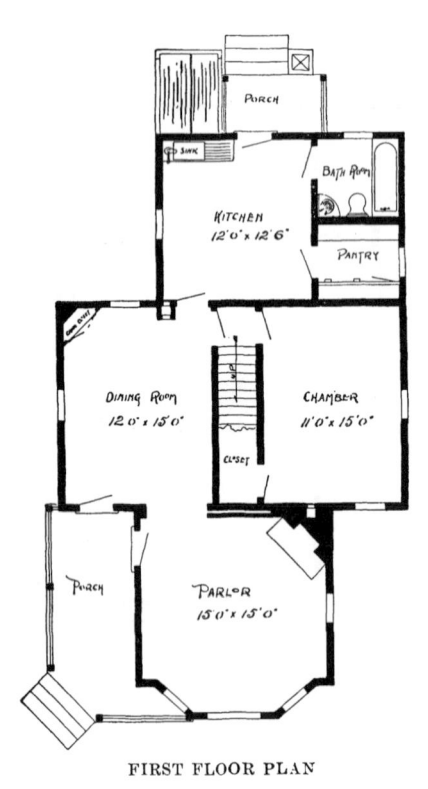

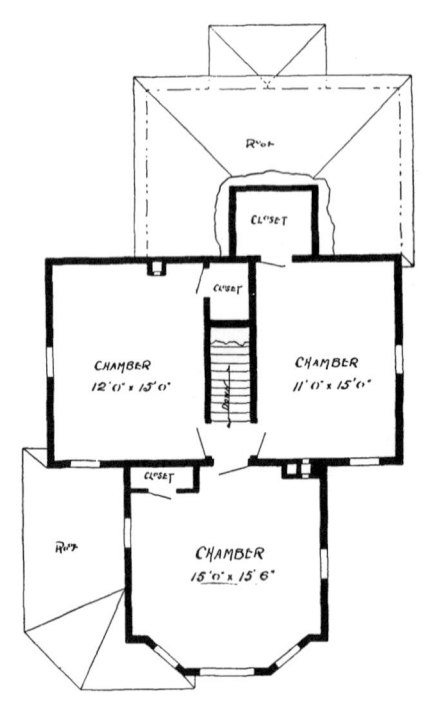

$5.00

FIRST FLOOR PLAN

SECOND FLOOR PLAN

Design No. 80
Cost about $1,700

Size : width, 28 feet ; length, 45 feet exclusive of porches. Blue prints consist of cellar and foundation plan; first and second floor plans; front, rear, two side elevations; wall sections and all necessary interior details.

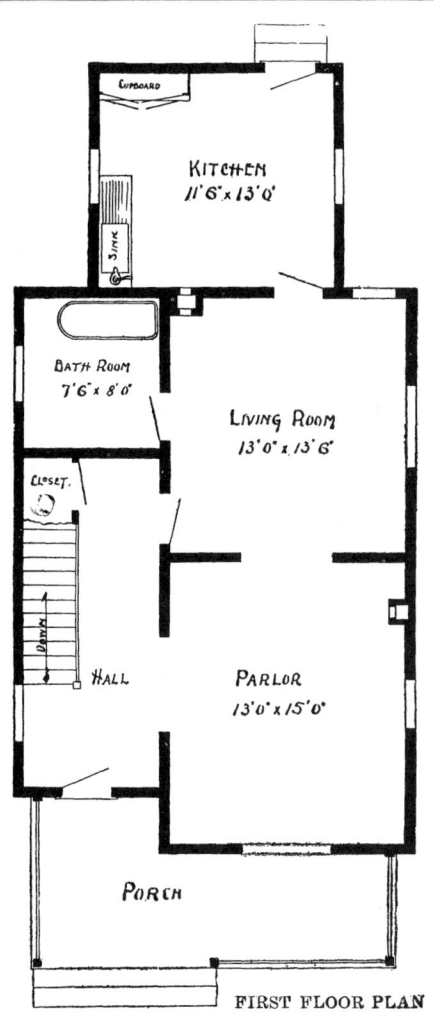

First Floor Plan

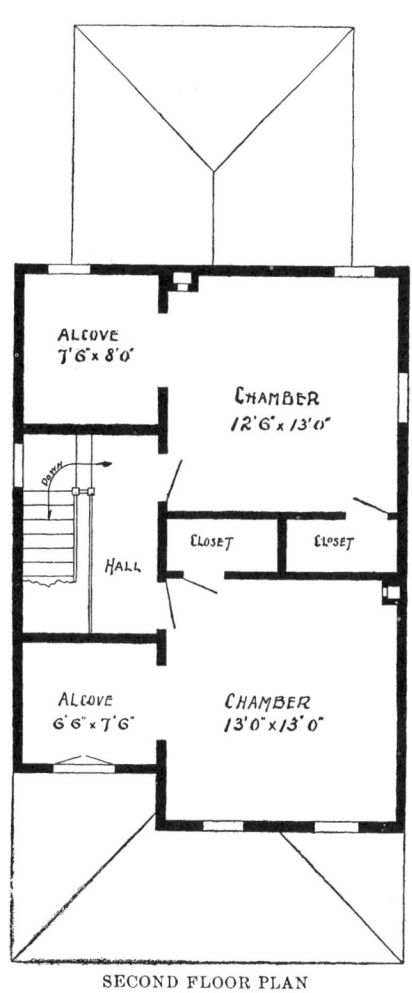

- Kitchen 11'6" x 13'0"
- Bath Room 7'6" x 8'0"
- Living Room 13'0" x 13'6"
- Closet
- Hall
- Parlor 13'0" x 15'0"
- Porch

Second Floor Plan

- Alcove 7'6" x 8'0"
- Chamber 12'6" x 13'0"
- Hall
- Closet | Closet
- Alcove 6'6" x 7'6"
- Chamber 13'0" x 13'0"

PRICE of Blue Prints, together with a complete set of typewritten specifications, is

$3.50

Size: width, 22 feet; length, 42 feet exclusive of porch. Blue prints consist of foundation plan; first and second floor plans; front, rear, two side elevations; wall sections and all necessary interior details.

Design No. 61
Cost about $750

PRICE of Blue Prints, together with a complete set of typewritten specifications, is

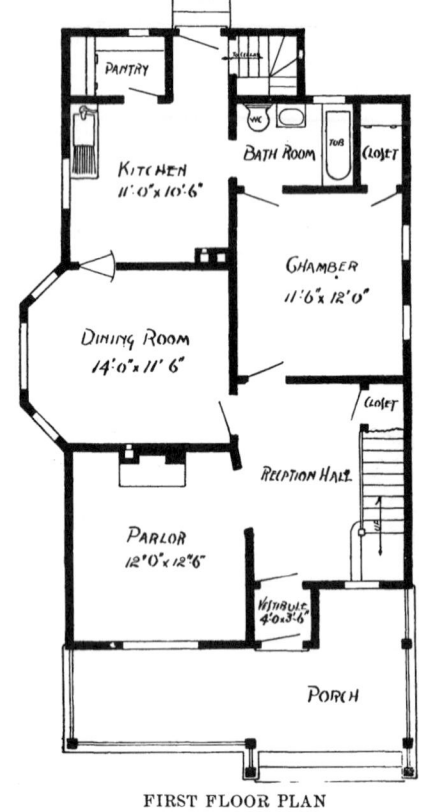

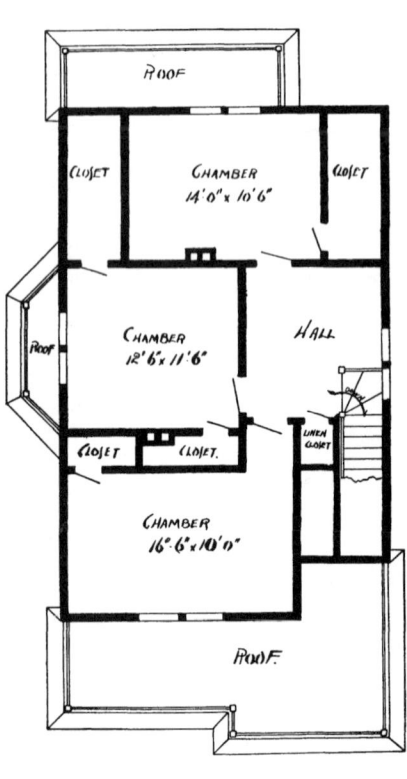

$5.00

FIRST FLOOR PLAN

SECOND FLOOR PLAN

Design No. 62
Cost about $1,600

Size: width, 27 feet; length, 41 feet exclusive of porch. Blue prints consist of cellar and foundation plan; first and second floor plans; front, rear, two side elevations; wall sections and all necessary interior details.

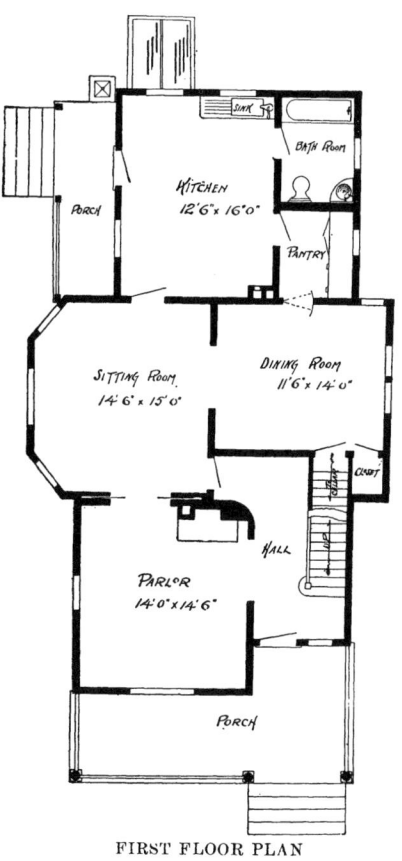

FIRST FLOOR PLAN

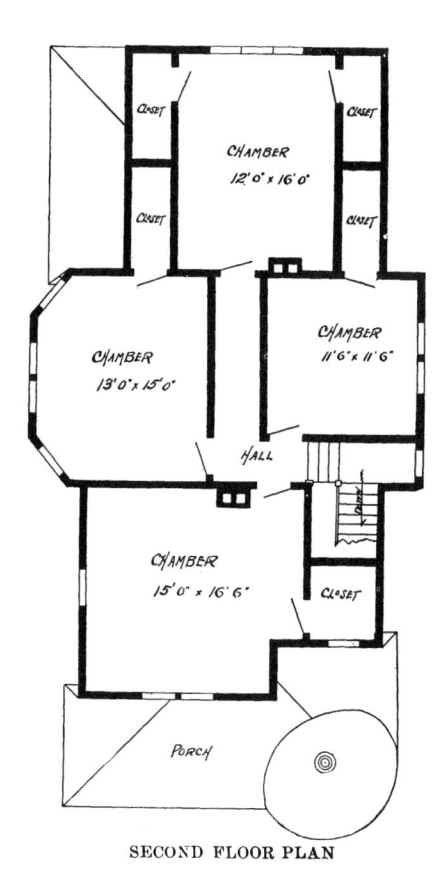

SECOND FLOOR PLAN

PRICE of Blue Prints together with a complete set of typewritten specifications, is

$5.00

Size: width, 30 feet; length, 48 feet exclusive of porch. Blue prints consist of cellar and foundation plan; first and second floor plans; front, rear, two side elevations; wall sections and all necessary interior details.

Design No. 83
Cost about $1,900

PRICE of Blue Prints, together with a complete set of typewritten specifications, is

$3.00

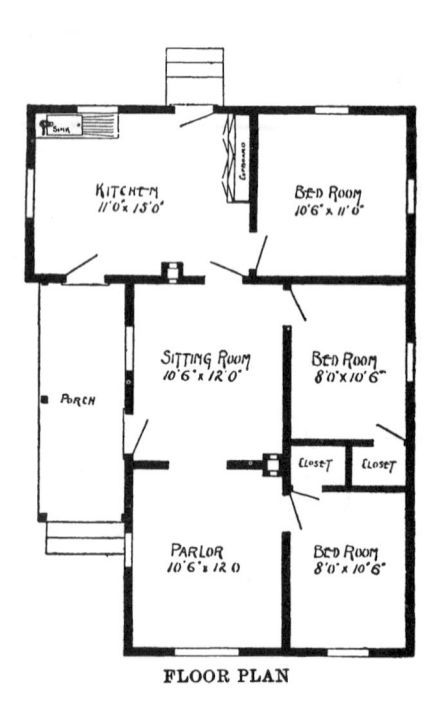

FLOOR PLAN

Design No. 51
Cost about $700

Size: width, 27 feet; length, 37 feet. Blue prints consist of foundation plan; floor plan; front, rear, two side elevations; wall sections and all necessary interior details.

PRICE
of Blue Prints, together with a complete set of typewritten specifications, is

$3.00

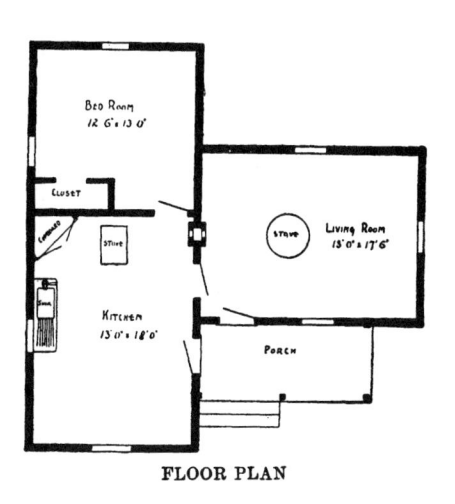

Size: width, 32 feet; length, 32 feet. Blue prints consist of foundation plan; floor plan; front, rear, two side elevations; wall sections and all necessary interior details.

FLOOR PLAN

Design No. 63
Cost about $500

47

PRICE of Blue Prints, together with a complete set of typewritten specifications, is

$5.00

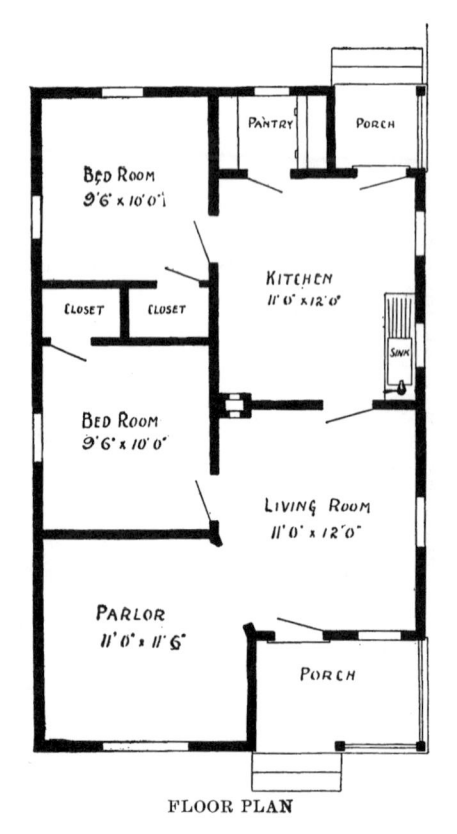

FLOOR PLAN

Design No. 64
Cost about $650

Size: width, 22 feet; length, 36 feet. Blue prints consist of foundation plan; floor plan; front, rear, two side elevations; wall sections and all necessary interior details.

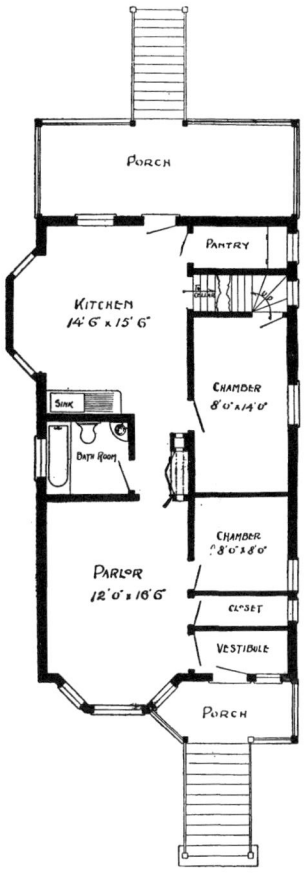

FLOOR PLAN

PRICE of Blue Prints, together with a complete set of typewritten specifications, is

$5.00

Size: width, 22 feet; length, 40 feet exclusive of porches. Blue prints consist of foundation plan; floor plan; front and side elevations; wall sections and all necessary interior details.

Design No. 79
Cost about $1,500

49

PRICE
of Blue Prints,
together with a
complete set of
typewritten
specifications, is

$3.00

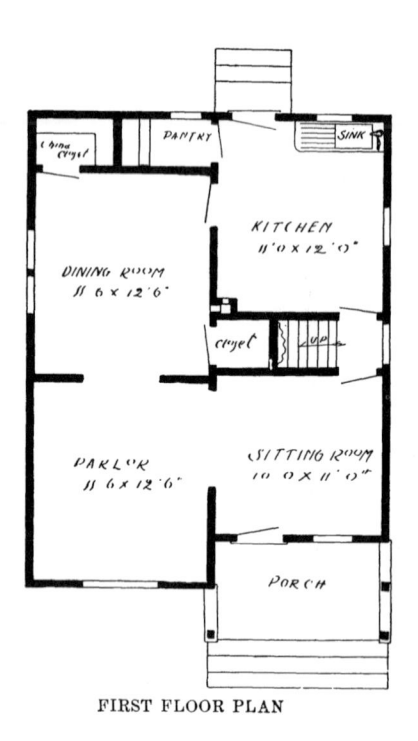

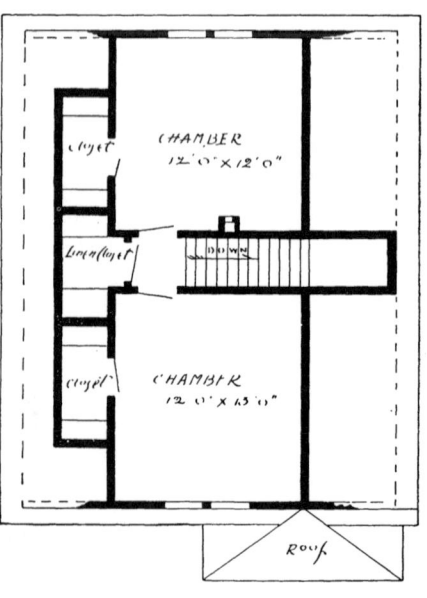

FIRST FLOOR PLAN

SECOND FLOOR PLAN

Design No. 3
Cost about $650

Size: width, 24 feet; length, 30 feet exclusive of porch. Blue prints consist of foundation plan; first and second floor plans; front, rear, two side elevations; wall sections and all necessary interior details.

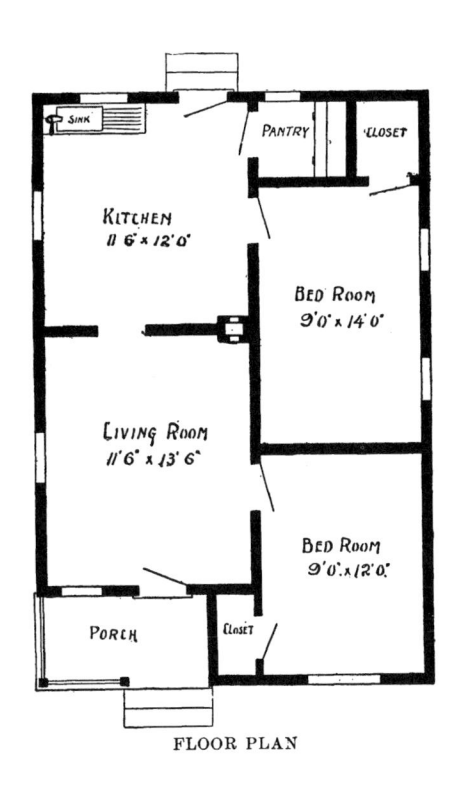

FLOOR PLAN

PRICE of Blue Prints, together with a complete set of typewritten specifications, is

$3.00

Size: width, 22 feet; length, 32 feet. Blue prints consist of foundation plan; floor plan; front, rear, two side elevations; wall sections and all necessary interior details.

Design No. 65
Cost about $575

51

PRICE of Blue Prints, together with a complete set of typewritten specifications, is

$4.00

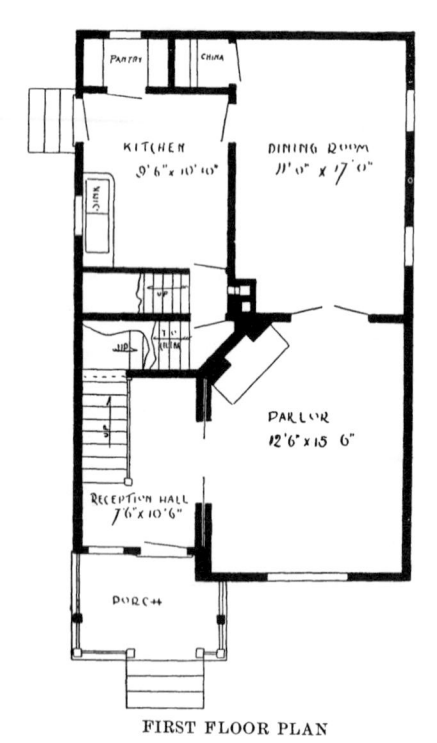

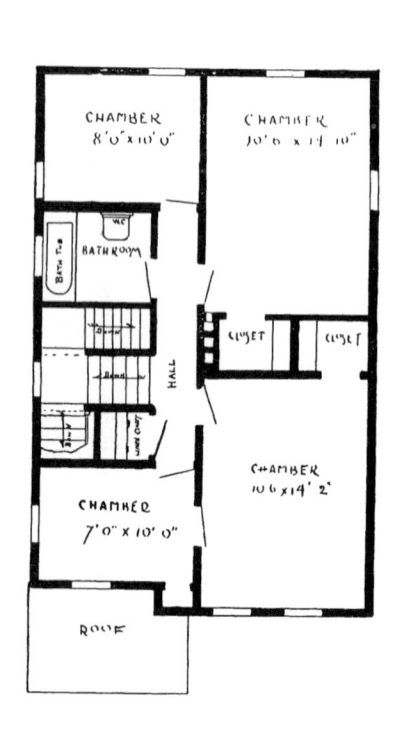

FIRST FLOOR PLAN

SECOND FLOOR PLAN

Design No. 8
Cost about $1,350

Size: width, 22 feet; length, 34 feet exclusive of porch. Blue prints consist of cellar and foundation plan; first and second floor plans; front, rear, two side elevations; wall sections and all necessary interior details.

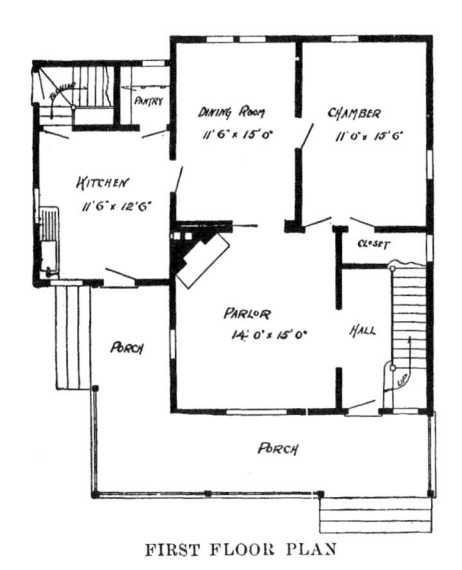

FIRST FLOOR PLAN

SECOND FLOOR PLAN

PRICE of Blue Prints, together with a complete set of typewritten specifications, is

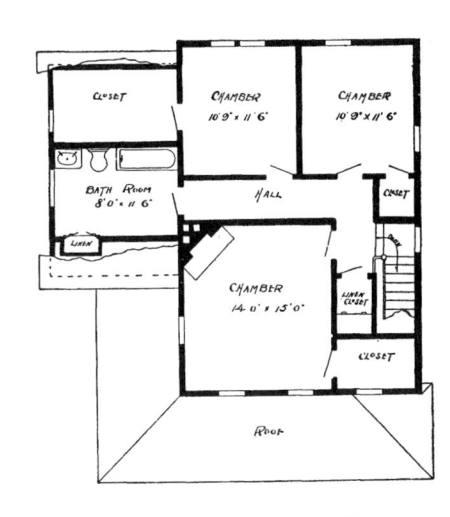

$5.⁰⁰

Size: width, 35 feet; length, 32 feet exclusive of porch. Blue prints consist of cellar and foundation plan; first and second floor plans; front, rear, two side elevations; wall sections and all necessary interior details.

Design No. 85
Cost about $1,400

PRICE of Blue Prints, together with a complete set of typewritten specifications, is

$3.00

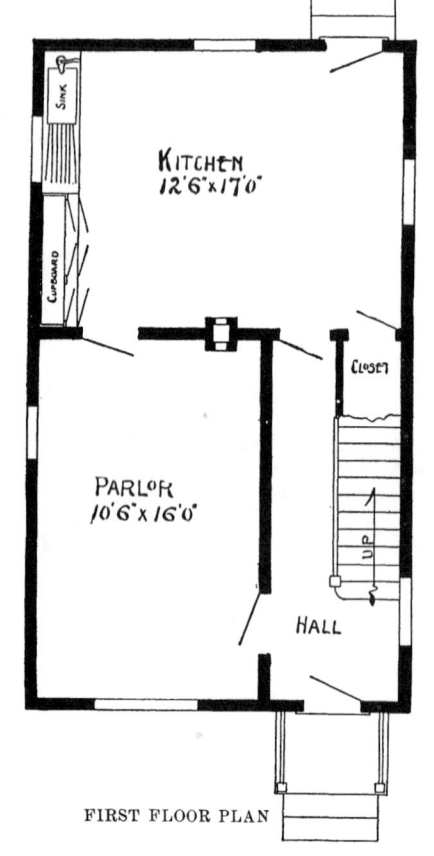

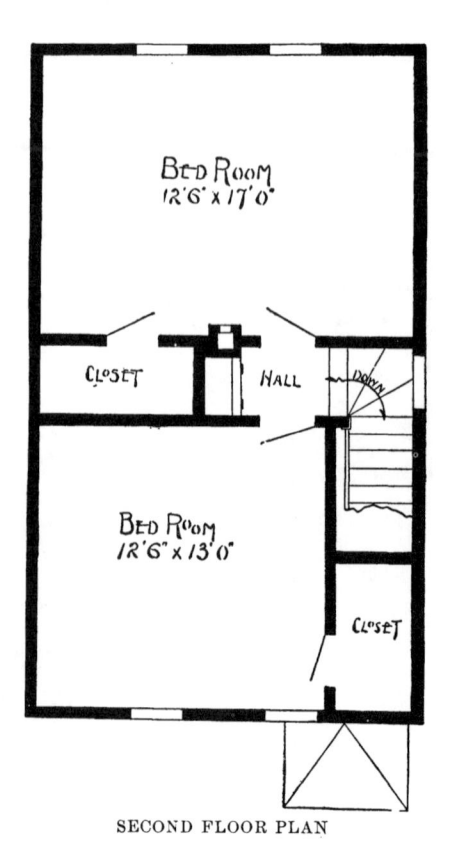

First Floor Plan
- Kitchen 12'6" x 17'0"
- Cupboard
- Sink
- Closet
- Parlor 10'6" x 16'0"
- Hall

Second Floor Plan
- Bed Room 12'6" x 17'0"
- Closet
- Hall
- Down
- Bed Room 12'6" x 13'0"
- Closet

Design No. 50
Cost about $650

Size: width, 18 feet; length, 30 feet exclusive of porch. Blue prints consist of foundation plan; first and second floor plans; front, rear, two side elevations; wall sections and all necessary interior details.

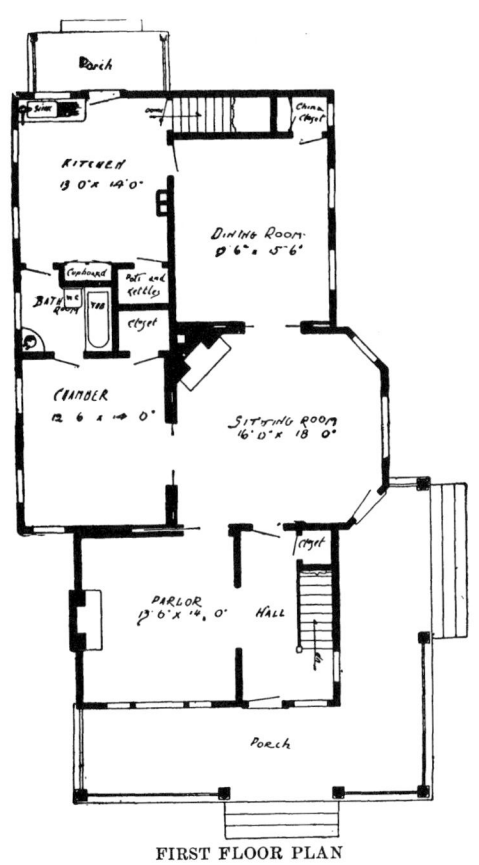

FIRST FLOOR PLAN

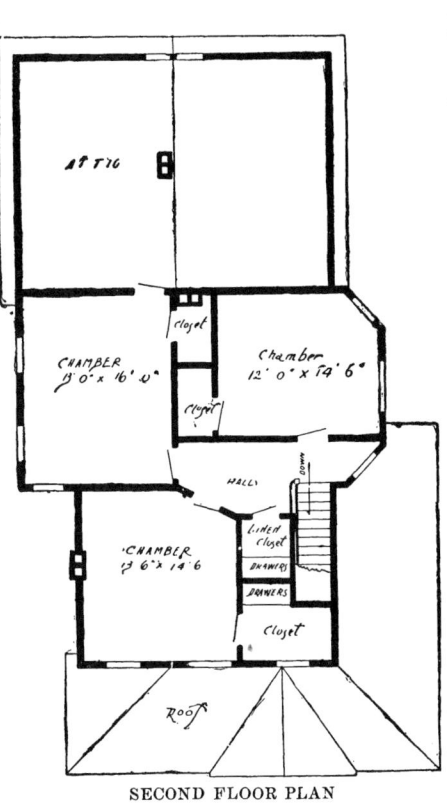

SECOND FLOOR PLAN

PRICE of Plue Prints, together with a complete set of typewritten specifications, is

$5.00

Size: width, 32 feet; length, 52 feet exclusive of porches. Blue prints consist of cellar and foundation plan; first and second floor plans; front, rear, two side elevations; wall sections and all necessary interior details.

Design No. 19
Cost about $1,900

55

PRICE of Blue Prints, **together** with a **complete** set of **typewritten** specifications, is

$3.00

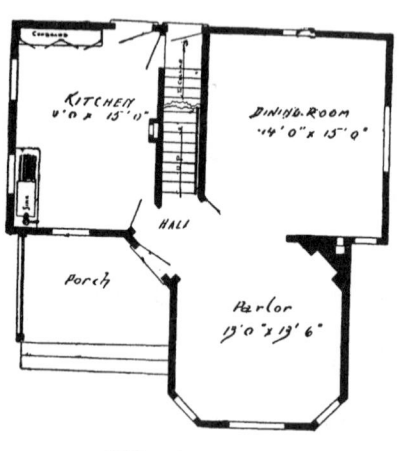

FIRST FLOOR PLAN

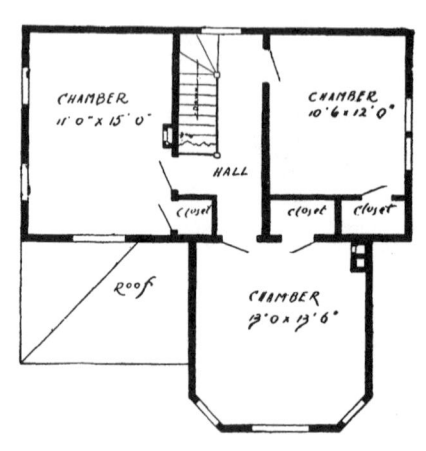

SECOND FLOOR PLAN

Design No. 21
Cost about $950

Size: width, 30 feet; length, 30 feet. Blue prints consist of cellar and foundation plan; first and second floor plans; front, rear, two side elevations; wall sections and all necessary interior details.

FIRST FLOOR PLAN

SECOND FLOOR PLAN

PRICE of Blue Prints, together with a complete set of typewritten specifications, is

$4.50

Size: width, 26 feet; length, 52 feet exclusive of porch. Blue prints consist of cellar and foundation plan; first and second floor plans; front, rear, two side elevations; wall sections and all necessary interior details.

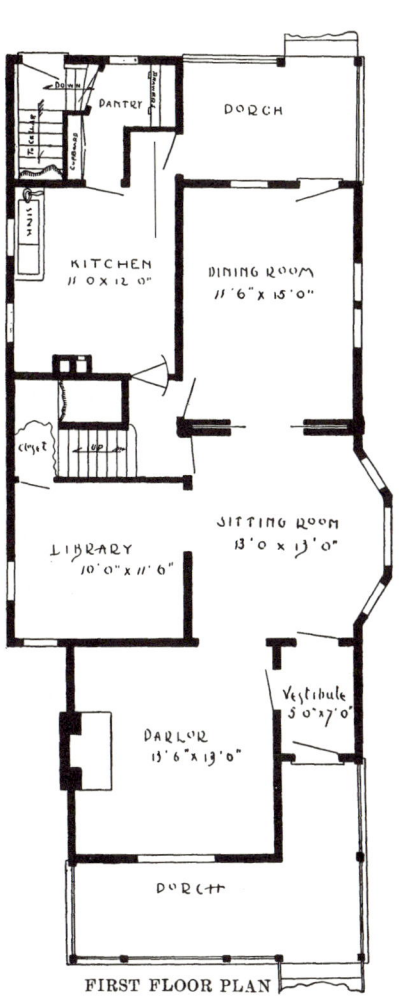

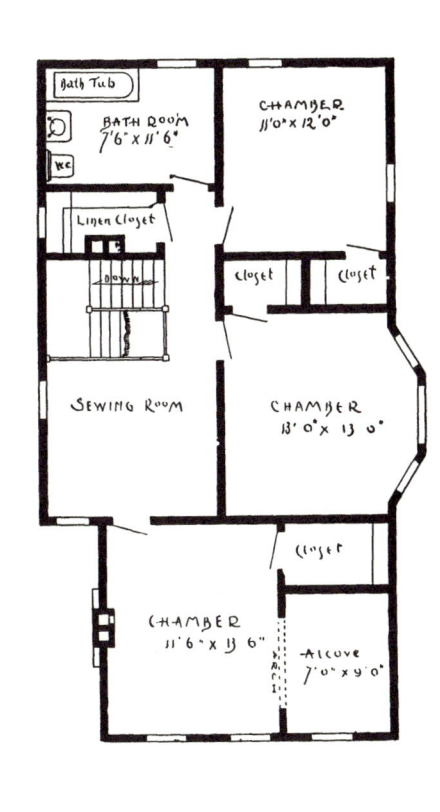

Design No. 11
Cost about $2,000

57

PRICE
of Blue Prints,
together with a
complete set of
typewritten
specifications, is

$4.00

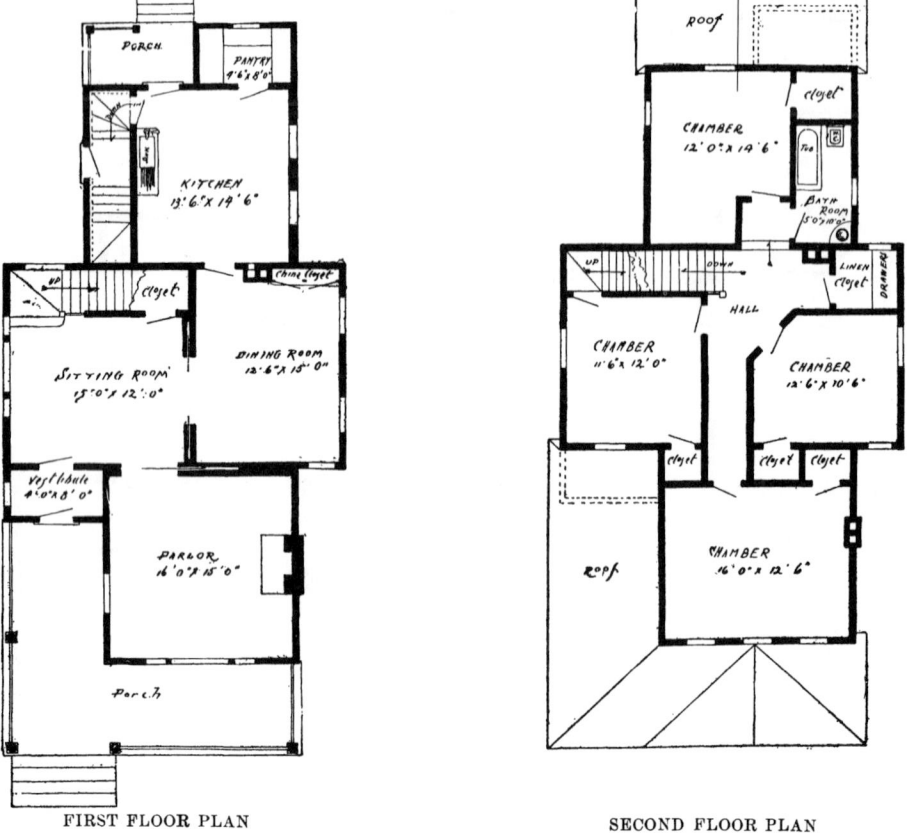

FIRST FLOOR PLAN

SECOND FLOOR PLAN

Design No. 18
Cost about $1,700

Size: width, 30 feet; length, 48 feet exclusive of porches. Blue prints consist of cellar and foundation plan; first and second floor plans; front, rear, two side elevations; wall sections and all necessary interior details.

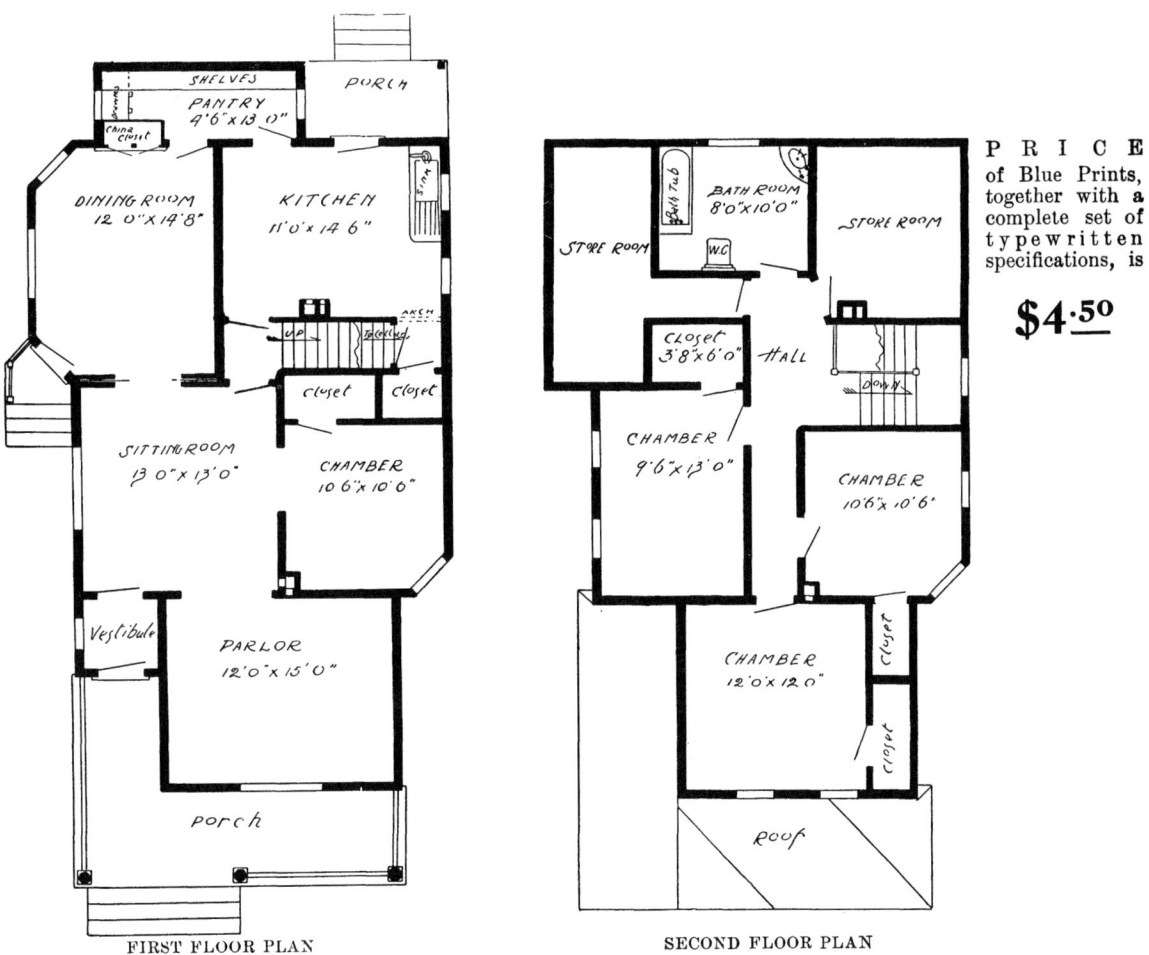

FIRST FLOOR PLAN

SECOND FLOOR PLAN

Size: width, 28 feet; length, 42 feet exclusive of porches. Blue prints consist of cellar and foundation plan; first and second floor plans; front, rear, two side elevations; wall sections and all necessary interior details.

PRICE of Blue Prints, together with a complete set of typewritten specifications, is

$4.50

Design No. 12
Cost about $1,700

59

PRICE of Blue Prints, together with a complete set of typewritten specifications, is

$3.50

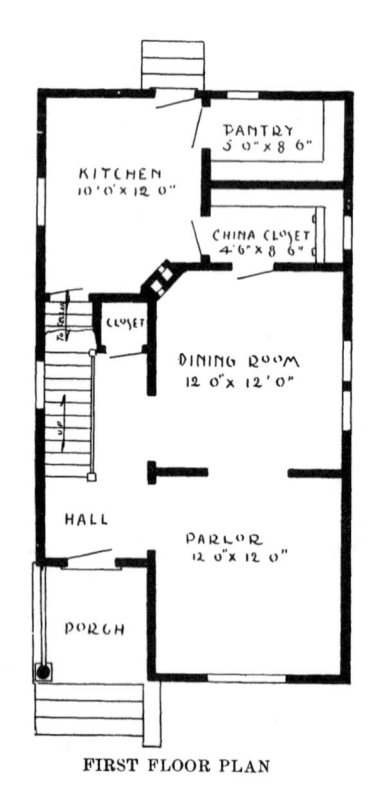

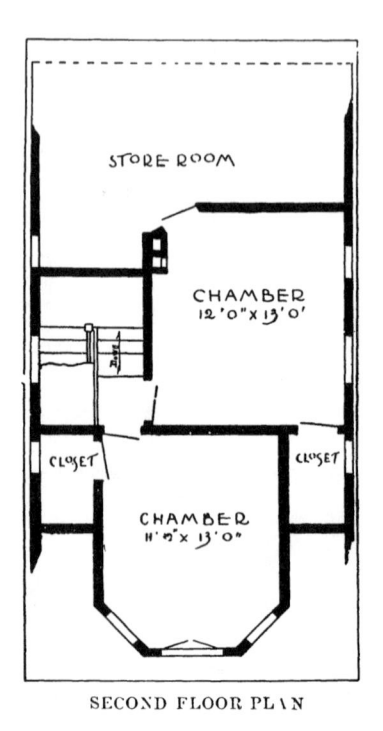

FIRST FLOOR PLAN

SECOND FLOOR PLAN

Design No. 4
Cost about $1,000

Size: width, 20 feet; length, 36 feet. Blue prints consist of cellar and foundation plan; first and second floor plans; front, **rear**, two side elevations; wall sections and all necessary interior details.

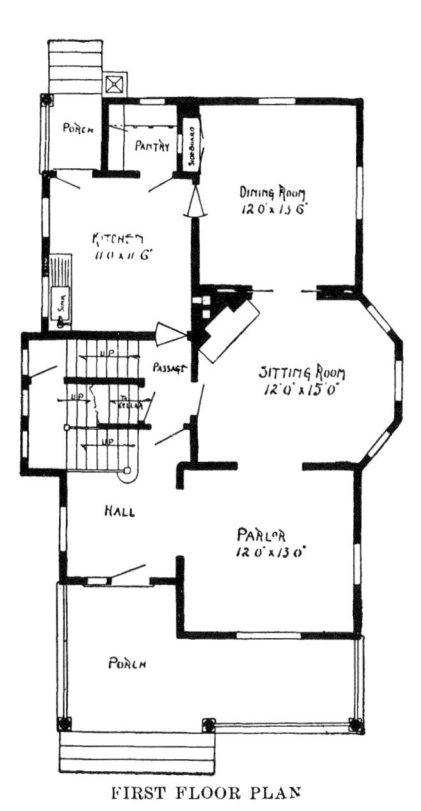

FIRST FLOOR PLAN

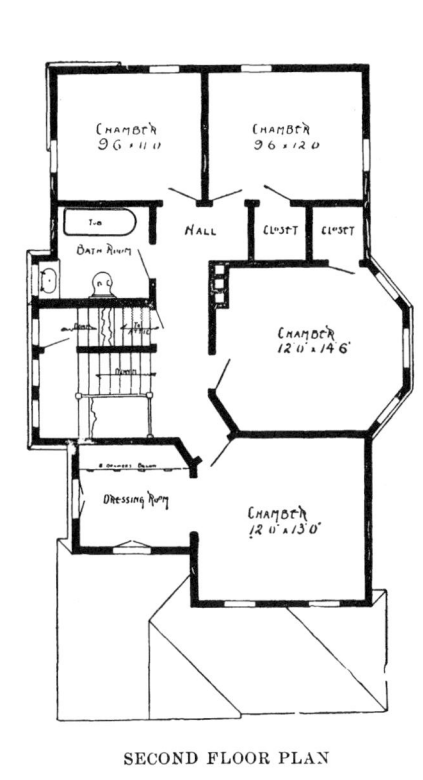

SECOND FLOOR PLAN

PRICE of Blue Prints, together with a complete set of typewritten specifications, is

$5.00

Size: width, 28 feet; length, 40 feet exclusive of porch. Blue prints consist of cellar and foundation plan; first and second floor plans; roof plan; front, rear, two side elevations; wall sections and all necessary interior details.

Design No. 54
Cost about $2,200

PRICE of Blue Prints, together with a complete set of typewritten specifications, is

$4.50

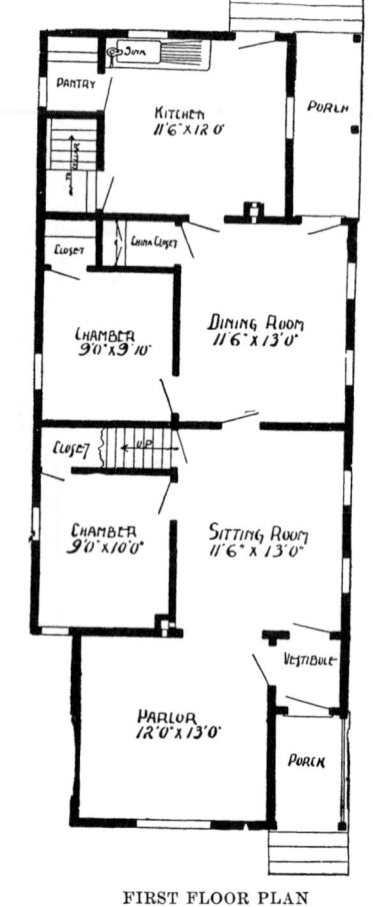

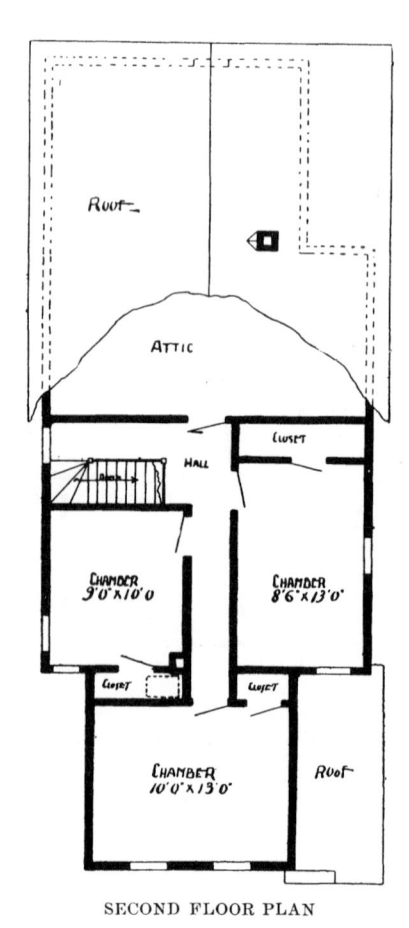

FIRST FLOOR PLAN

SECOND FLOOR PLAN

Design No. 44
Cost about $1,600

Size: width, 22 feet; length, 52 feet. Blue prints consist of cellar and foundation plan; first and second floor plans; front, rear, two side elevations; wall sections and all necessary interior details.

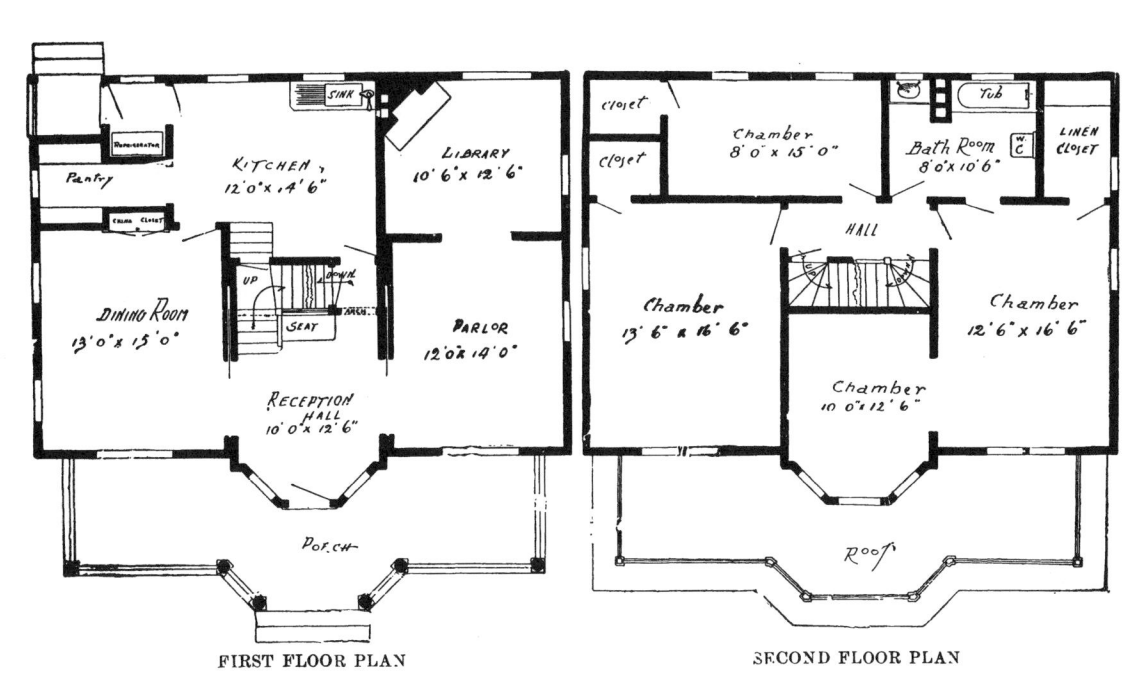

FIRST FLOOR PLAN

SECOND FLOOR PLAN

PRICE of Blue Prints, together with a complete set of typewritten specifications, is

$4.50

Size: width, 38 feet; length, 26 feet exclusive of porches. Blue prints consist of cellar and foundation plan; first and second floor plans; front, rear, two side elevations; wall sections and all necessary interior details.

Design No. 26
Cost about $1,800

PRICE of Blue Prints, together with a complete set of typewritten specifications, is

$7.50

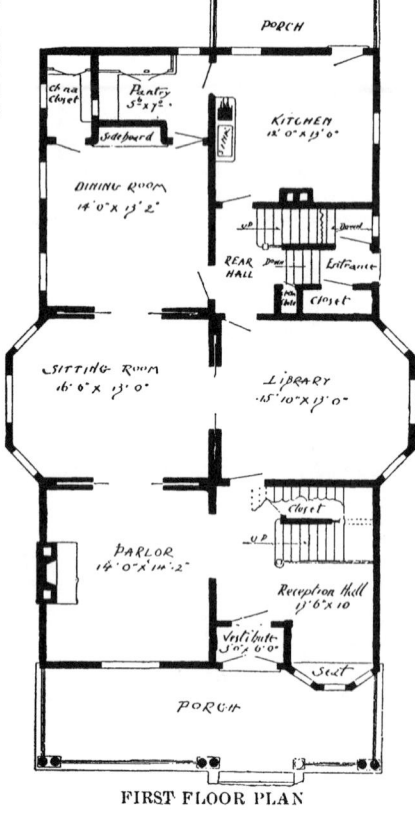

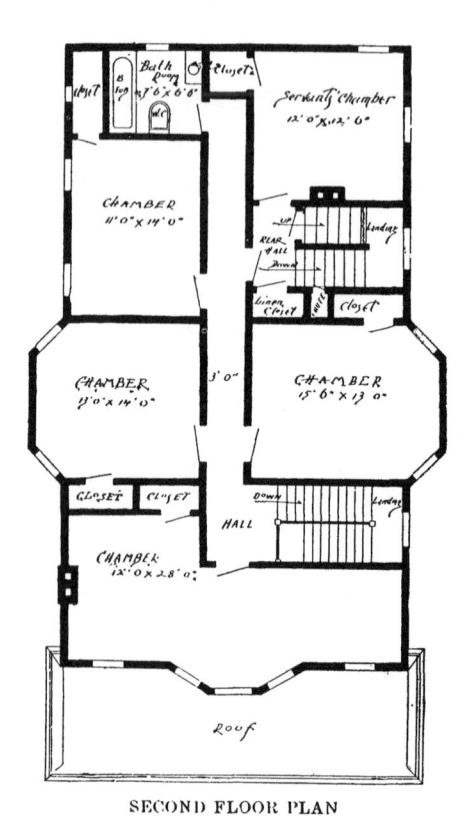

FIRST FLOOR PLAN   SECOND FLOOR PLAN

Design No. 15
Cost about $3,700

Size: width, 34 feet; length, 50 feet exclusive of porches. Blue prints consist of cellar and foundation plan; first and second floor plans; front, rear, two side elevations; wall sections and all necessary interior details.

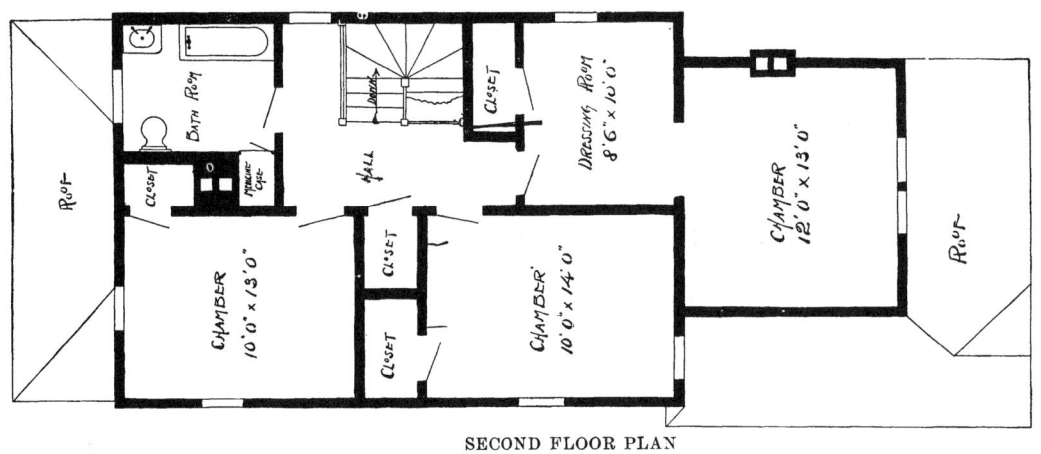

SECOND FLOOR PLAN

FIRST FLOOR PLAN

PRICE of Blue Prints, together with a complete set of typewritten specifications, is

$5.00

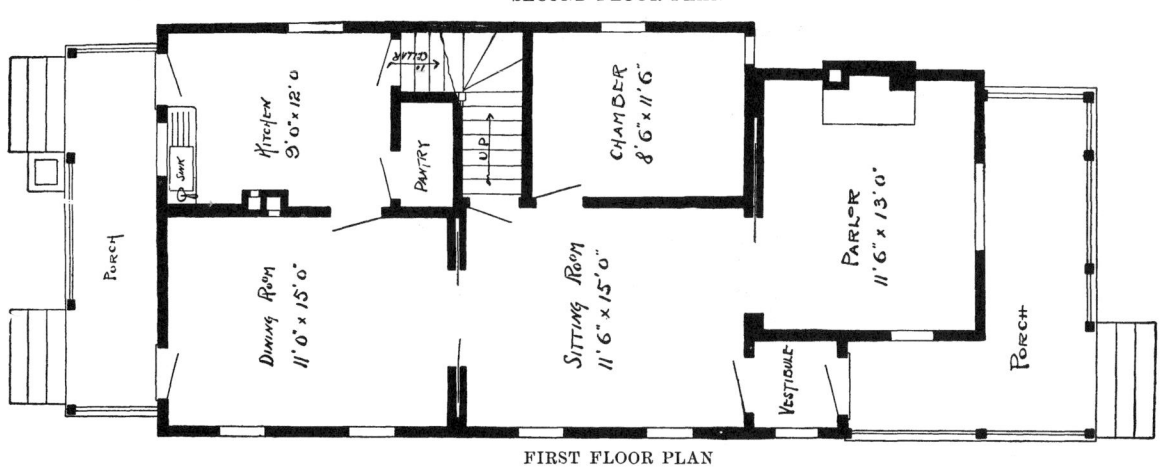

Size: width, 21 feet 6 inches; length, 44 feet 6 inches exclusive of porches. Blue prints consist of cellar and foundation plan; first and second floor plans; front, rear, two side elevations; wall sections and all necessary interior details.

Design No. 98
Cost about $1,800

PRICE of Blue Prints, together with a complete set of typewritten specifications, is

$3.00

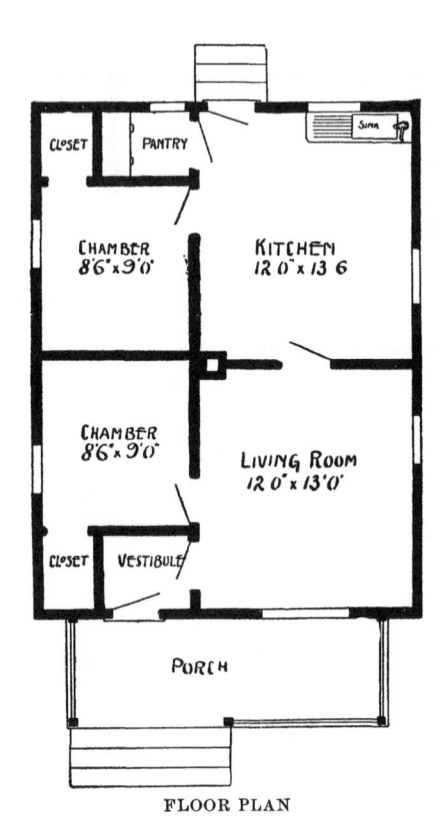

FLOOR PLAN

Design No. 46
Cost about $550

Size: width, 22 feet; length, 28 feet exclusive of porch. Blue prints consist of foundation plan; floor plan; front, rear, two side elevations; wall sections and all necessary interior details.

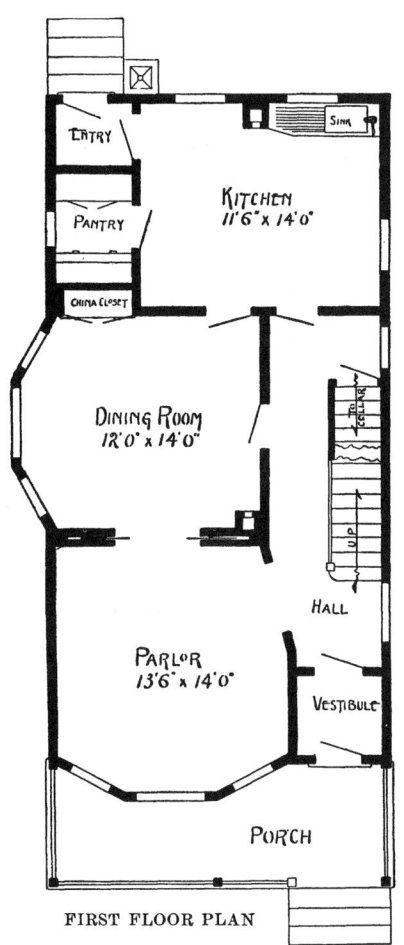

FIRST FLOOR PLAN

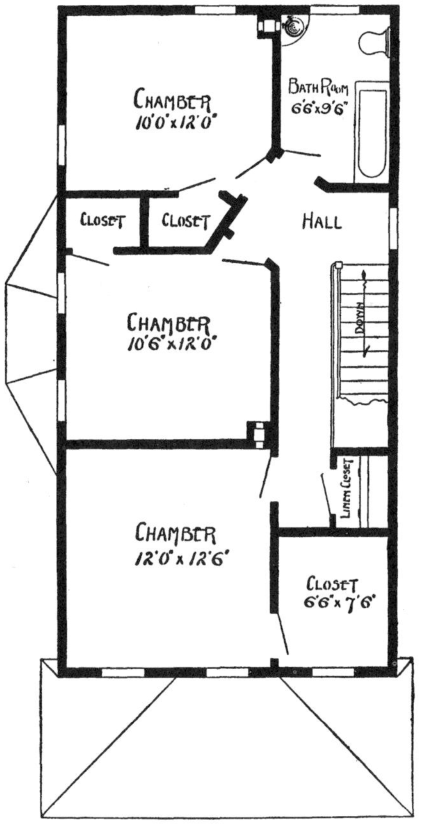

- Entry
- Kitchen 11'6" x 14'0"
- Pantry
- China Closet
- Dining Room 12'0" x 14'0"
- Hall
- Parlor 13'6" x 14'0"
- Vestibule
- Porch

SECOND FLOOR PLAN

- Chamber 10'0" x 12'0"
- Bath Room 6'6" x 9'6"
- Closet
- Closet
- Hall
- Chamber 10'6" x 12'0"
- Chamber 12'0" x 12'6"
- Linen Closet
- Closet 6'6" x 7'6"

PRICE of Blue Prints, together with a complete set of typewritten specifications, i

$4.00

Size: width, 22 feet; length, 40 feet exclusive of porch. Blue prints consist of cellar and foundation plan; first and second floor plans; front, rear, two side elevations; wall sections and all necessary interior details.

Design No. 47
Cost about $1,350

67

PRICE of Blue Prints, together with a complete set of typewritten specifications, is

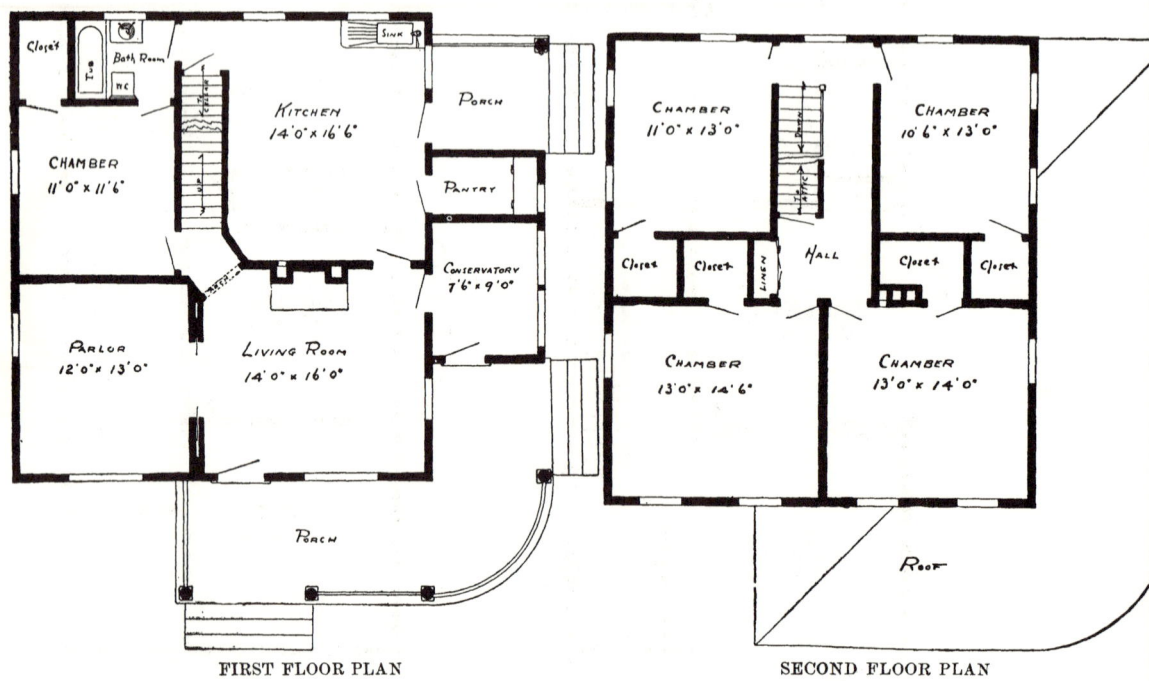

$5.00

FIRST FLOOR PLAN

SECOND FLOOR PLAN

Design No. 23
Cost about $2,000

Size: width, 30 feet; length, 32 feet exclusive of porches. Blue prints consist of cellar and foundation plan; first and second floor plans; front, rear, two side elevations · wall sections and all necessary interior details.

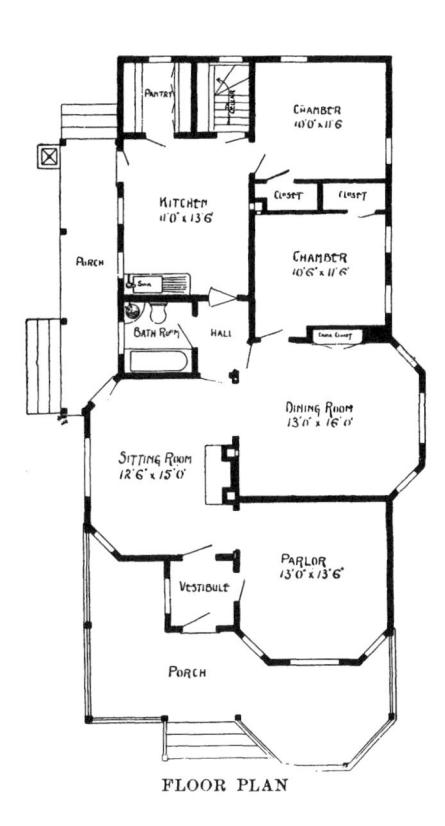

FLOOR PLAN

PRICE of Blue Prints, together with a complete set of typewritten specifications, is

$5.00

Size: width, 30 feet; length, 52 feet exclusive of porches. Blue prints consist of cellar and foundation plan; floor and roof plans; front, rear, two side elevations; wall sections and all necessary interior details.

Design No. 49
Cost about $1,500

PRICE of Blue Prints, together with a complete set of typewritten specifications, is

$3.⁰⁰

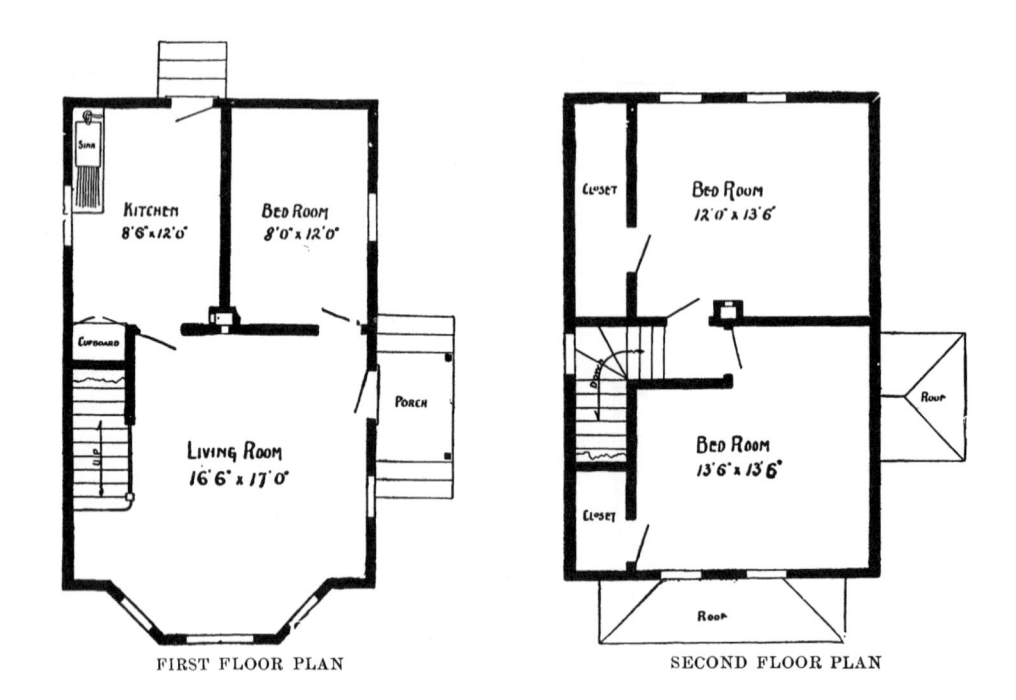

FIRST FLOOR PLAN

- Kitchen 8'6" x 12'0"
- Bed Room 8'0" x 12'0"
- Cupboard
- Porch
- Living Room 16'6" x 17'0"

SECOND FLOOR PLAN

- Closet
- Bed Room 12'0" x 13'6"
- Bed Room 13'6" x 13'6"
- Closet
- Roof
- Roof

Design No. 58
Cost about $600

Size: width, 18 feet; length, 30 feet exclusive of porch. Blue prints consist of foundation plan; first and second floor plans; front, rear, two side elevations; wall sections and all necessary interior details.

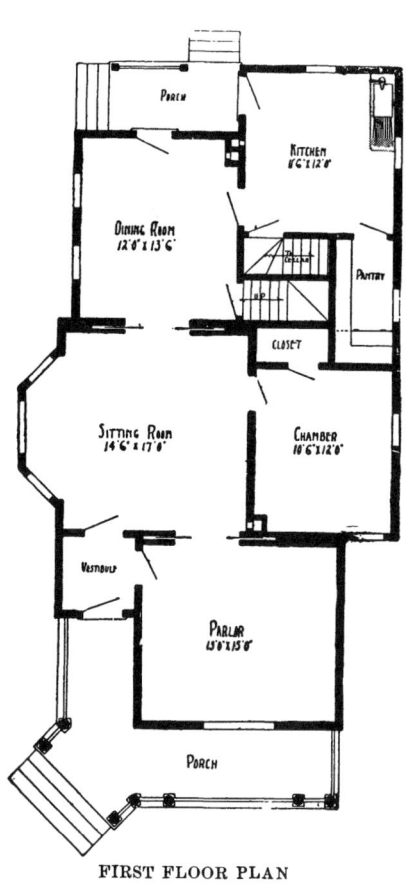

FIRST FLOOR PLAN

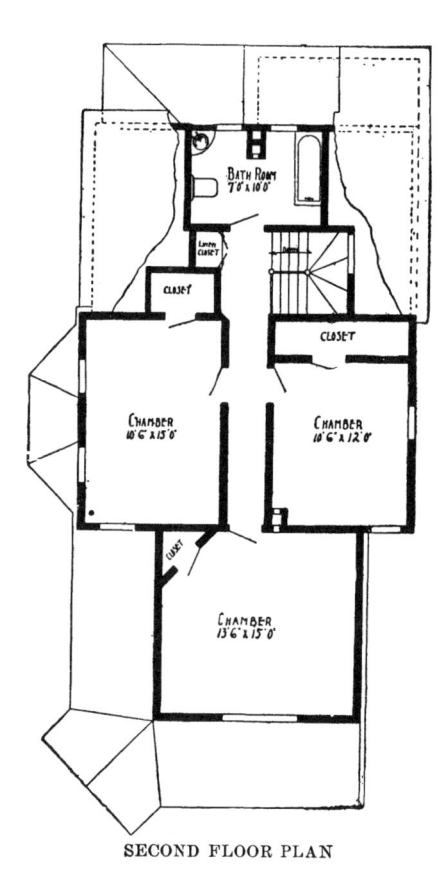

SECOND FLOOR PLAN

PRICE of Blue Prints, together with a complete set of typewritten specifications, is

$5.00

Size: width, 29 feet; length, 49 feet exclusive of porches. Blue prints consist of cellar and foundation plan; first and second floor plans; front, rear, two side elevations; wall sections and all necessary interior details.

Design No. 40
Cost about $2,000

71

FIRST FLOOR PLAN   SECOND FLOOR PLAN

PRICE of Blue Prints, together with a complete set of typewritten specifications, is **$8.00**

Design No. 87
Cost about $2,700

Size: width, 40 feet; length, 67 feet exclusive of porch. Blue prints consist of foundation plan; first and second floor plans; front, rear, two side elevations; wall sections and all necessary interior details.

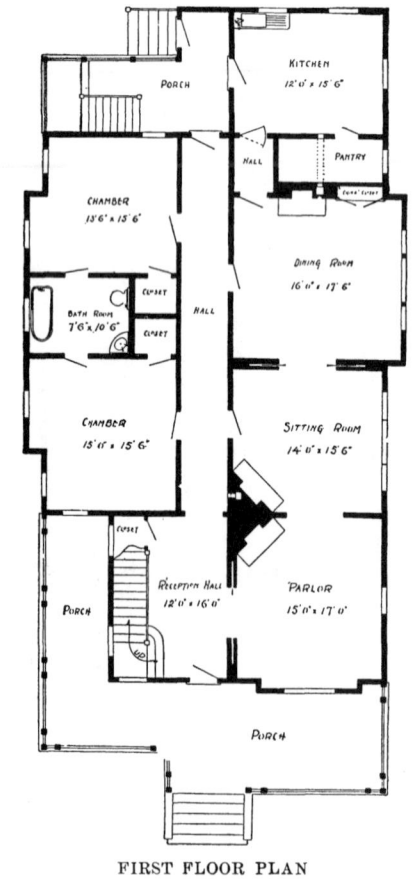

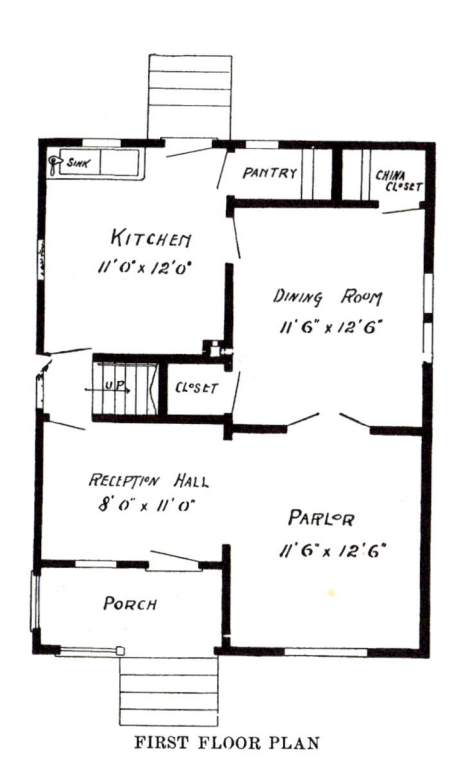

FIRST FLOOR PLAN

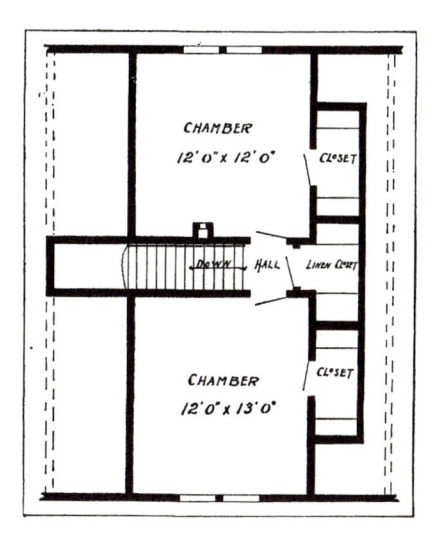

SECOND FLOOR PLAN

PRICE of Blue Prints, together with a complete set of typewritten specifications, is

$4.00

Size: width, 21 feet; length, 30 feet exclusive of porches. Blue prints consist of cellar and foundation plan; first and second floor plans; front, **rear,** two side elevations; wall sections and all necessary interior details.

Design No. 90
Cost about $800

PRICE of Blue Prints, together with a complete set of typewritten specifications, is

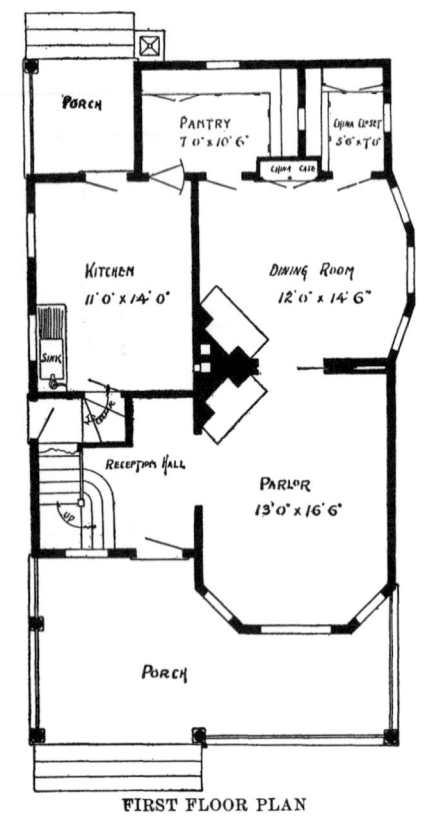

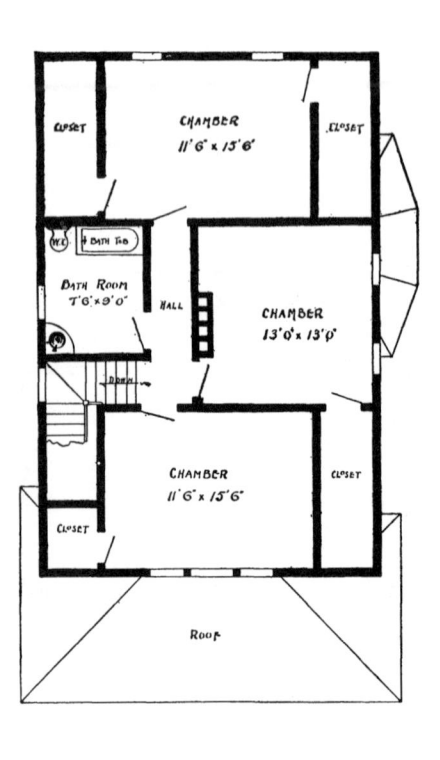

$5.00

FIRST FLOOR PLAN

SECOND FLOOR PLAN

Design No. 68
Cost about $1,550

Size: width, 27 feet; length, 38 feet exclusive of porches. Blue prints consist of cellar and foundation plan; first and second floor plans; front, rear, two side elevations; wall sections and all necessary interior details.

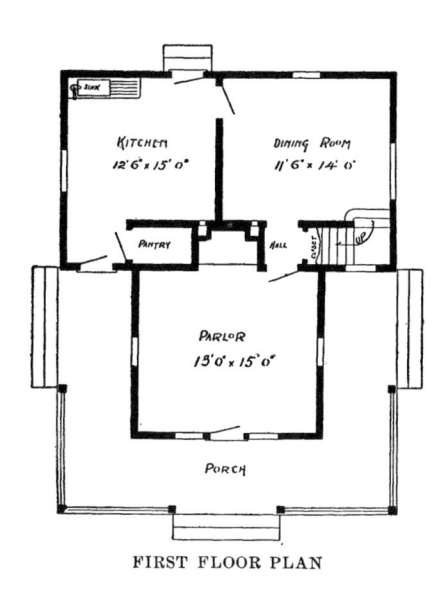

FIRST FLOOR PLAN

SECOND FLOOR PLAN

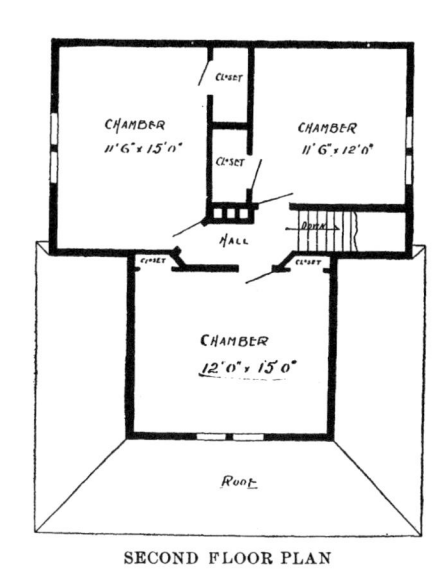

PRICE of Blue Prints, together with a complete set of typewritten specifications, is

$5.00

Size: width, 28 feet; length, 29 feet 6 inches exclusive of porch. Blue prints consist of foundation plan; first and second floor plans; front, rear, two side elevations; wall sections and all necessary interior details.

Design No. 88
Cost about $800

PRICE of Blue Prints, together with a complete set of typewritten specifications, is

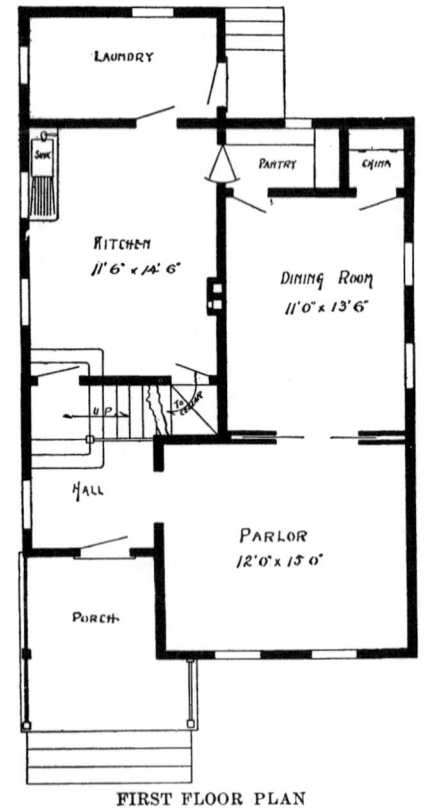

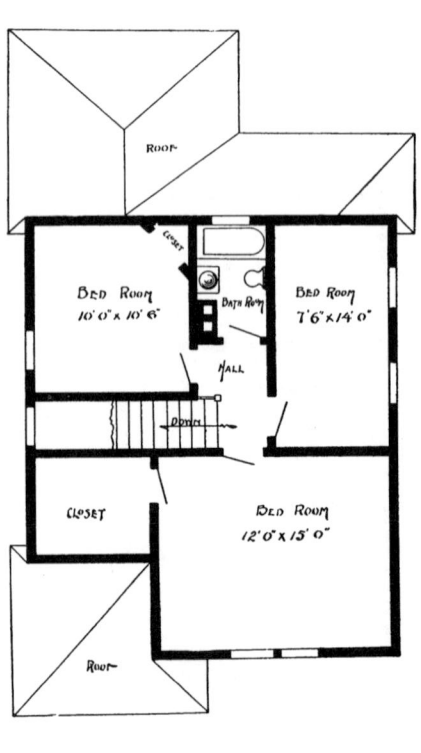

$5.00

FIRST FLOOR PLAN

SECOND FLOOR PLAN

Design No. 67
Cost about $1,000

Size: width, 24 feet; length, 40 feet exclusive of porch. Blue prints consist of cellar and foundation plan; first and second floor plans; front, rear, two side elevations; wall sections and all necessary interior details.

76

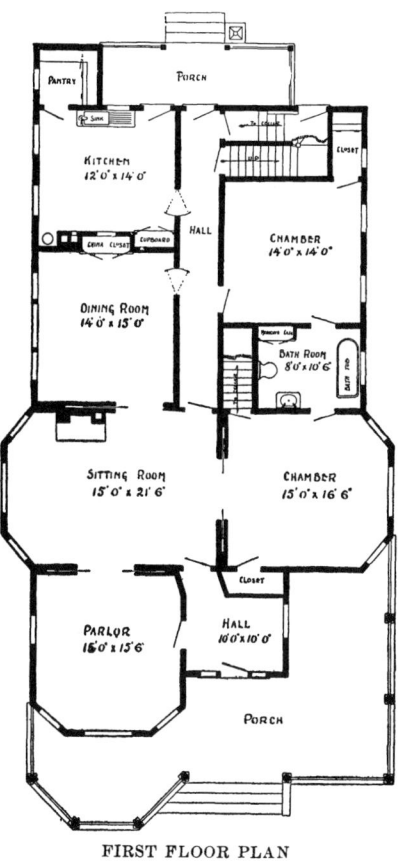

FIRST FLOOR PLAN

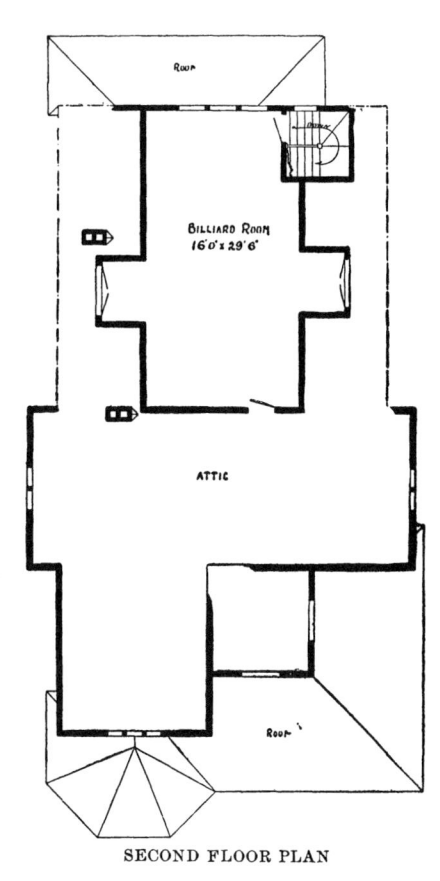

SECOND FLOOR PLAN

PRICE of Blue Prints, together with a complete set of typewritten specifications, is

$6.00

Size: width, 40 feet; length, 62 feet 6 inches exclusive of porches. Blue prints consist of cellar and foundation plan; first and second floor plans; front, rear, two side elevations; wall sections and all necessary interior details.

Design No. 70
Cost about $1,800

PRICE of Blue Prints, together with a complete set of typewritten specifications, is

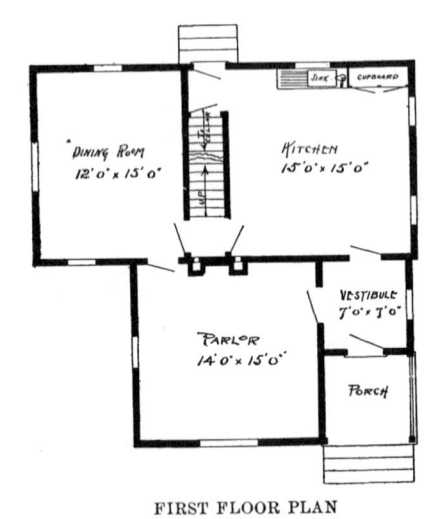

$5.00

FIRST FLOOR PLAN

SECOND FLOOR PLAN

Design No. 93
Cost about $1,200

Size: width, 32 feet; length, 31 feet exclusive of porch. Blue prints consist of cellar and foundation plan; first and second floor plans; front, rear, two side elevations; wall sections and all necessary interior details

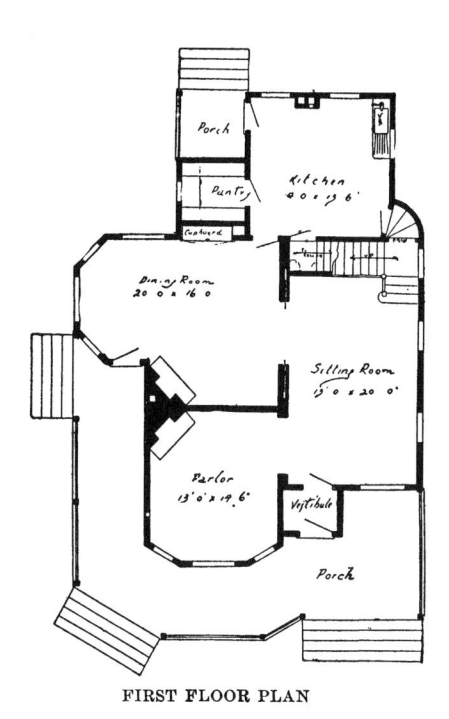

FIRST FLOOR PLAN

SECOND FLOOR PLAN

PRICE of Blue Prints, together with a complete set of typewritten specifications, is

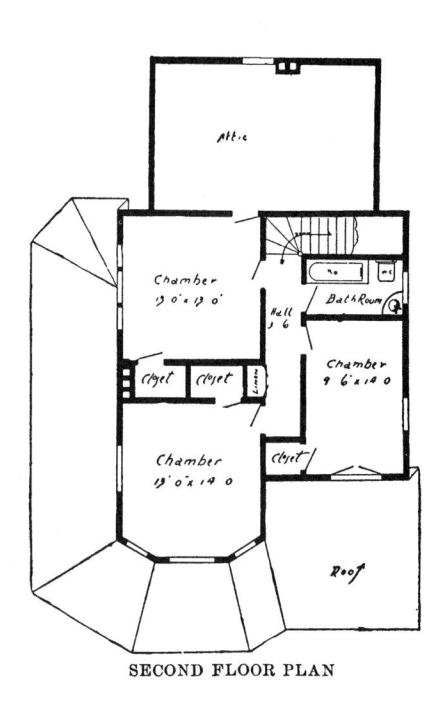

$5.00

Size: width, 35 feet; length, 46 feet exclusive of porches. Blue prints consist of cellar and foundation plan; first and second floor plans; front, rear, two side elevations; wall sections and all necessary interior details

Design No. 25
Cost about $1,900

PRICE of Blue Prints, together with a complete set of typewritten specifications, is

$5.00

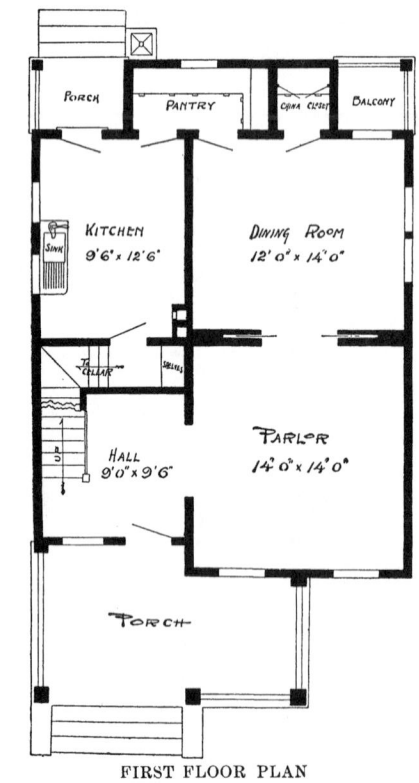

FIRST FLOOR PLAN

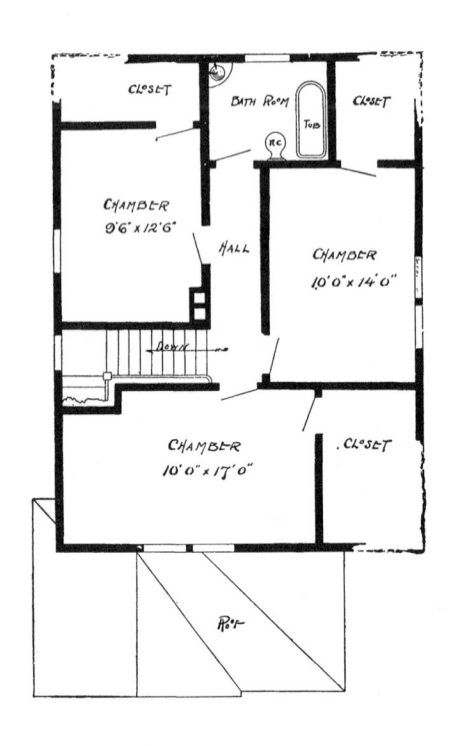

SECOND FLOOR PLAN

Design No. 95
Cost about $1,250

Size: width, 25 feet; length, 32 feet exclusive of porches. Blue prints consist of cellar and foundation plan; first and second floor plans; front, rear, two side elevations; wall sections and all necessary interior details.

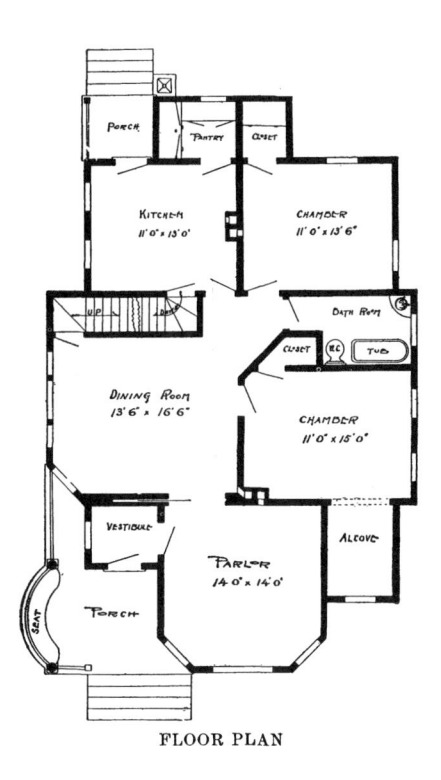

FLOOR PLAN

PRICE of Blue Prints, together with a complete set of typewritten specifications, is

$5.00

Size: width, 33 feet; length, 50 feet. Blue prints consist of foundation plan; floor plan; front, rear, two side elevations; wall sections and all necessary interior details.

Design No. 96
Cost about $1,250

PRICE of Blue Prints, together with a complete set of typewritten specifications, is

$4.00

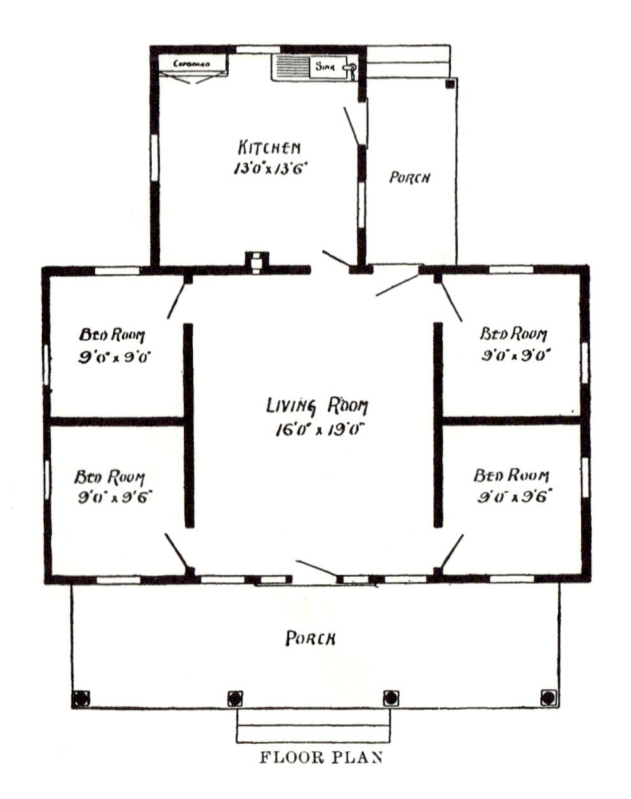

Floor Plan
- Kitchen 13'0" x 13'6"
- Porch
- Bed Room 9'0" x 9'0"
- Bed Room 9'0" x 9'0"
- Living Room 16'0" x 19'0"
- Bed Room 9'0" x 9'6"
- Bed Room 9'0" x 9'6"
- Porch

FLOOR PLAN

Design No. 55
Cost about $550

Size: width, 36 feet; length, 34 feet exclusive of porches. Blue prints consist of foundation plan; floor plan; front, rear, two side elevations; wall section and all necessary interior details.

82

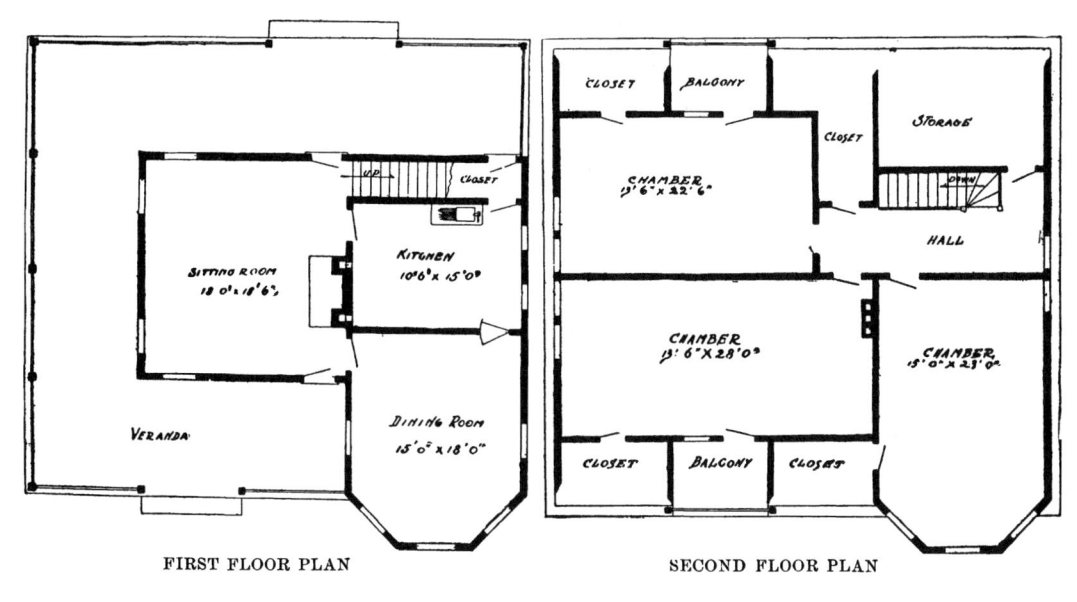

FIRST FLOOR PLAN

SECOND FLOOR PLAN

PRICE of Blue Prints, together with a complete set of typewritten specifications, is

$5.00

Size: width, 44 feet; length, 34 feet. Blue prints consist of foundation plan; first and second floor plans; front, rear, two side elevations; wall sections and all necessary interior details.

Design No. 27
Cost about $1,500

83

PRICE of Blue Prints, together with a complete set of typewritten specifications, is

$3.00

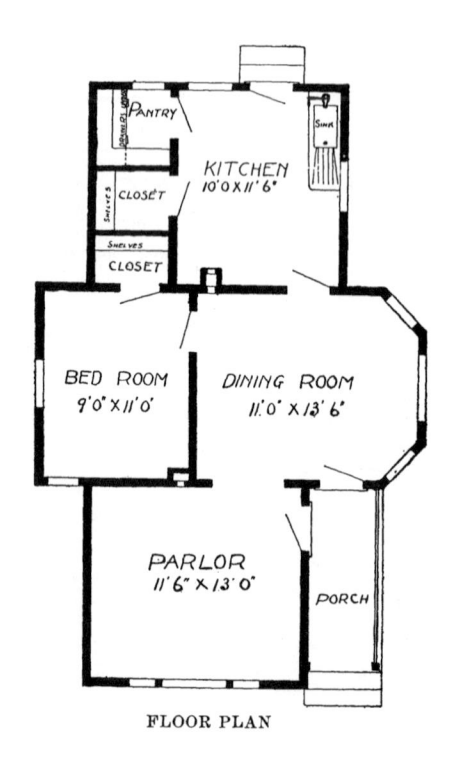

Design No. 32
Cost about $600

Size: width, 24 feet; length, 36 feet. Blue prints consist of foundation plan; floor plan; front, rear, two side elevations; wall sections and all necessary interior details.

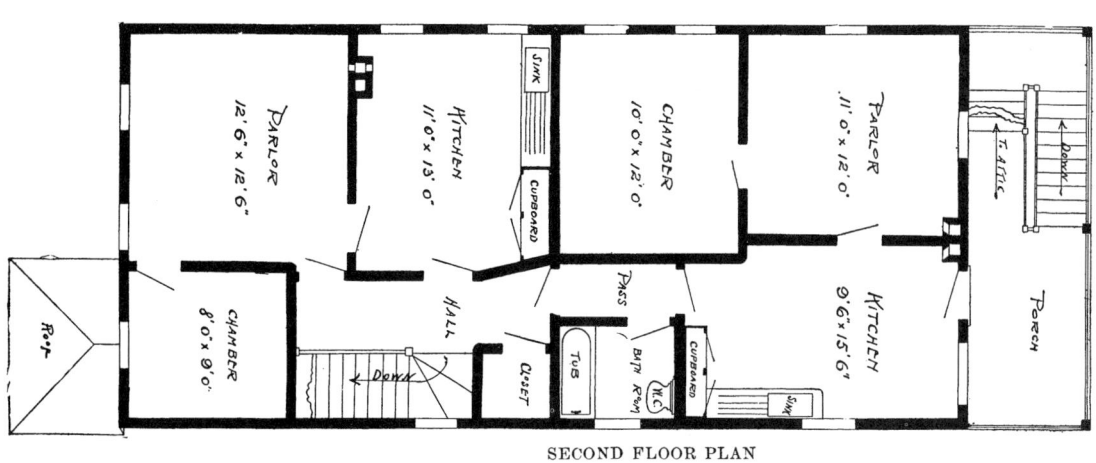

PRICE of Blue Prints, together with a complete set of typewritten specifications, is

$5.00

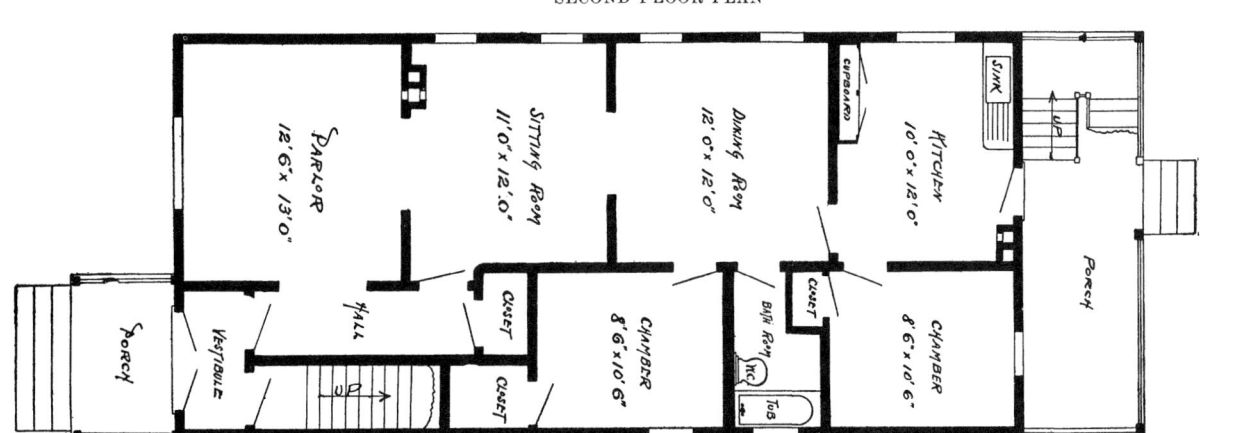

SECOND FLOOR PLAN

FIRST FLOOR PLAN

Size: width, 22 feet; length, 48 feet exclusive of porch. Blue prints consist of cellar and foundation plan; first and second floor plans; front, rear, two side elevations; wall sections and all necessary interior details.

Design No. 94
Cost about $2,000

PRICE of Blue Prints, together with a complete set of typewritten specifications, is

$5.00

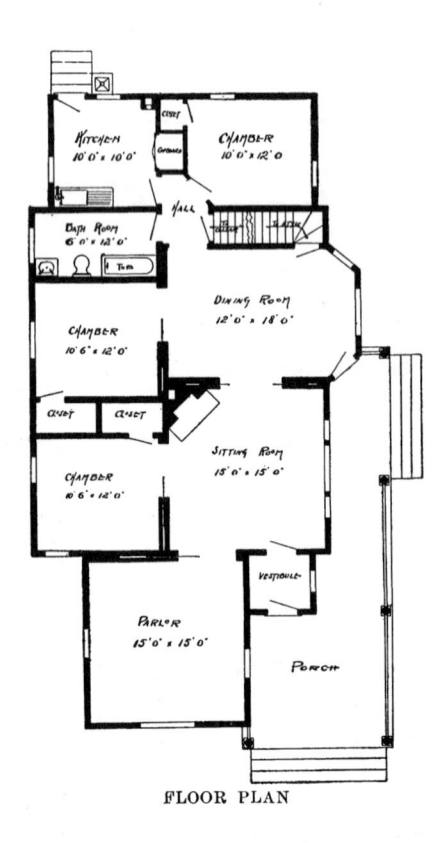

Design No. 99
Cost about $1,600

Size: width, 32 feet; length, 59 feet. Blue prints consist of cellar and foundation plan; floor plan; front, rear, two side elevations; wall sections and all necessary interior details.

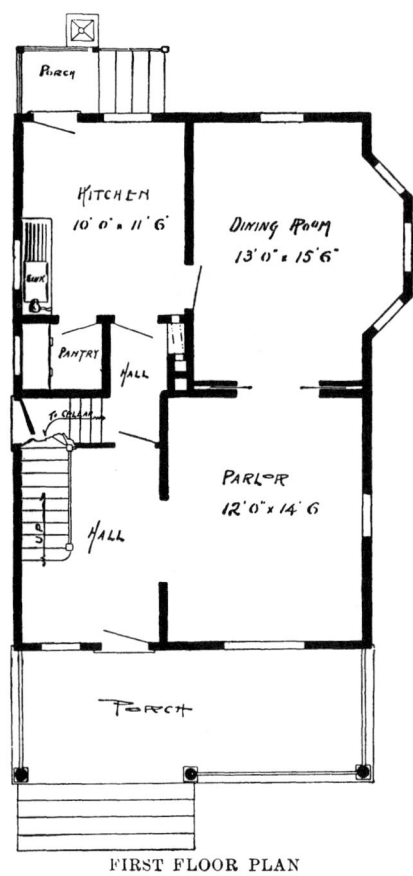

FIRST FLOOR PLAN

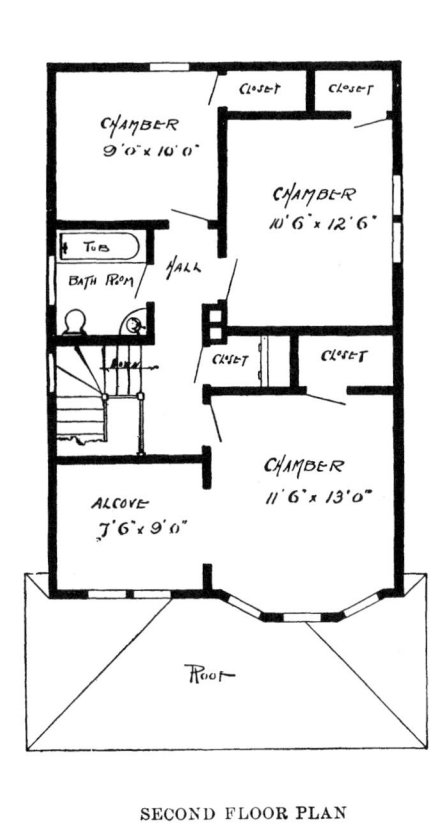

SECOND FLOOR PLAN

PRICE of Blue Prints, together with a complete set of typewritten specifications, is

$5.00

Size: width, 24 feet; length, 32 feet exclusive of porches. Blue prints consist of cellar and foundation plan; floor plans; front, rear, two side elevations; wall sections and all necessary interior details.

Design No. 100
Cost about $1,500

87

PRICE of Blue Prints, together with a complete set of typewritten specifications, is

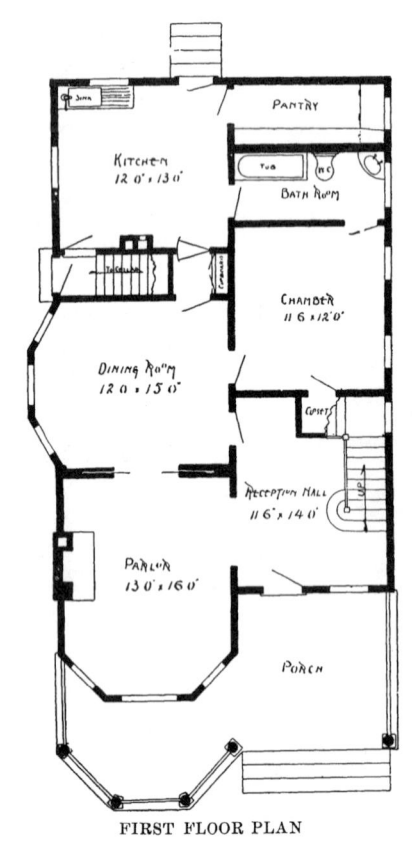

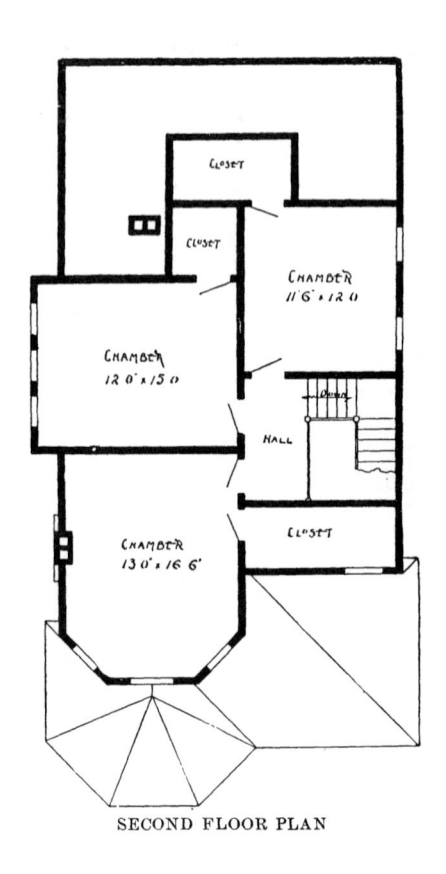

$5.00

FIRST FLOOR PLAN

SECOND FLOOR PLAN

Design No. 53
Cost about $2,200

Size : width, 28 feet; length, 46 feet exclusive of porch. Blue prints consist of cellar and foundation plan; first and second floor plans; roof plan; front, rear, two side elevations; wall sections and all necessary interior details.

FIRST FLOOR PLAN　　　　　SECOND FLOOR PLAN

Size: width, 25 feet; length, 40 feet exclusive of porches. Blue prints consist of cellar and foundation plan; first and second floor plans; roof and attic plan; front, rear, two side elevations; wall sections and all necessary interior details.

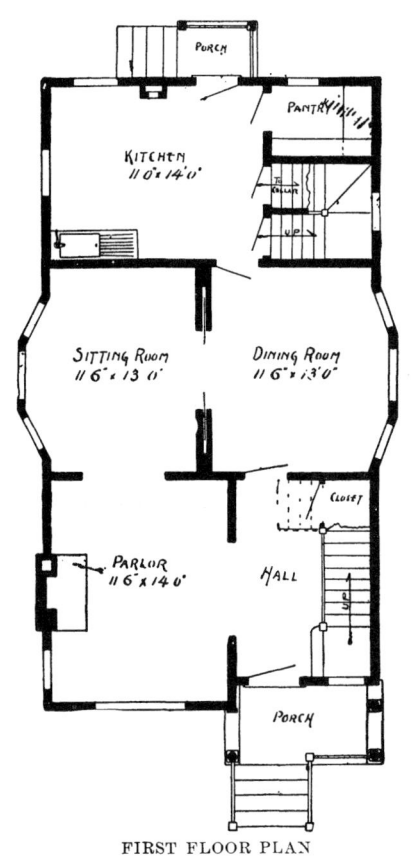

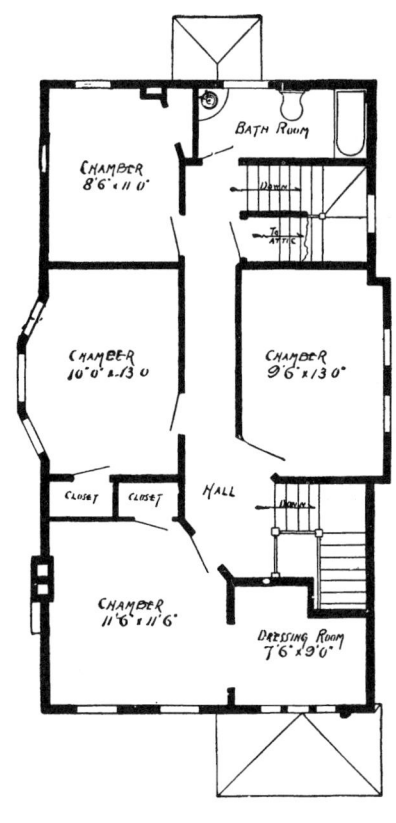

PRICE of Blue Prints, together with a complete set of typewritten specifications, is

$5.00

Design No. 52
Cost about $2,000

89

PRICE of Blue Prints, together with a complete set of typewritten specifications, is

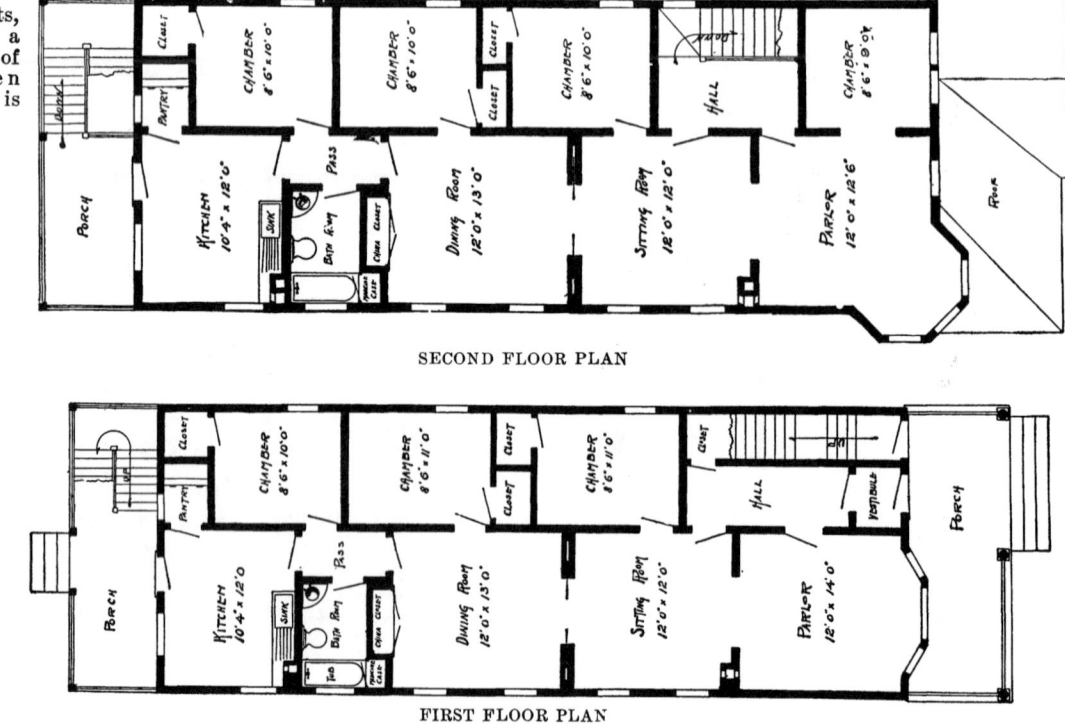

$5.00

SECOND FLOOR PLAN

FIRST FLOOR PLAN

Design No. 101
Cost about $2,200

Size: width, 22 feet; length, 60 feet exclusive of porches. Blue prints consist of foundation plan; first and second floor plans; front, rear, two side elevations; wall sections and all necessary interior details.

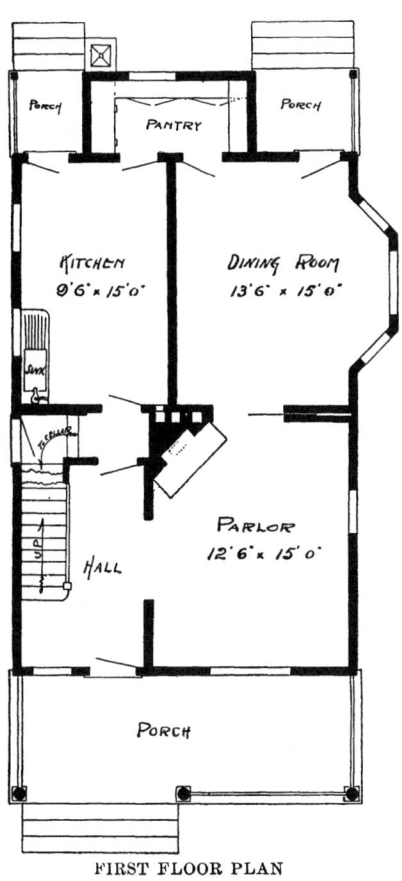

FIRST FLOOR PLAN

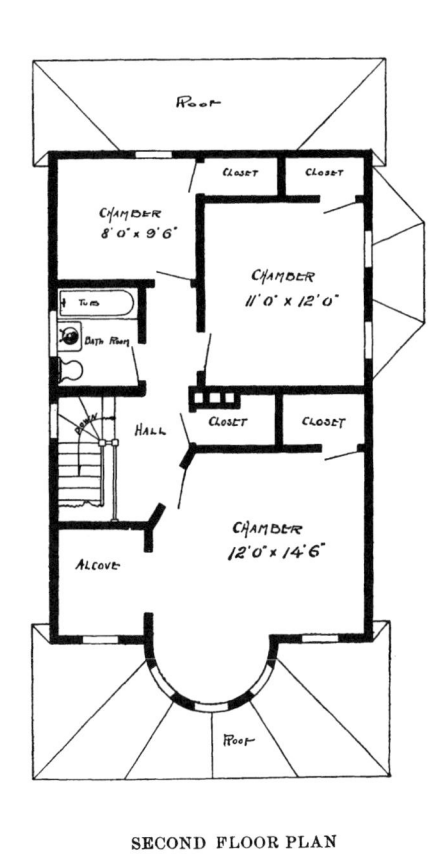

SECOND FLOOR PLAN

PRICE of Blue Prints, together with a complete set of typewritten specifications, is

$5.00

Size: width, 24 feet 6 inches; length, 37 feet exclusive of porches. Blue prints consist of cellar and foundation plan; first and second floor plans; front, rear, two side elevations; wall sections and all necessary interior details.

Design No. 102
Cost about $1,500

PRICE of Blue Prints, together with a complete set of typewritten specifications, is

$5.00

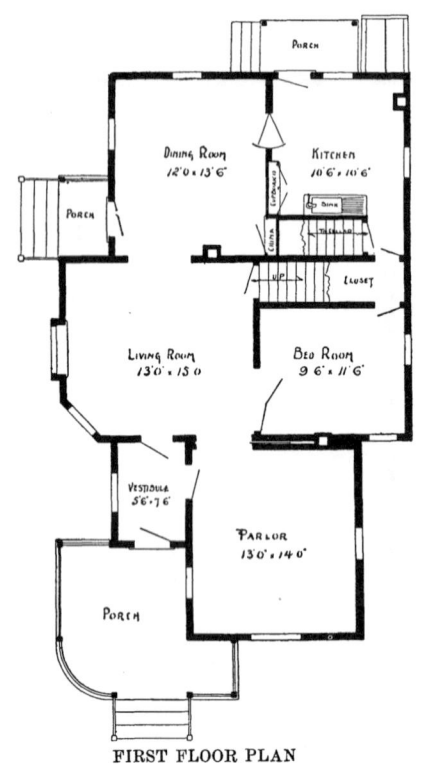

FIRST FLOOR PLAN

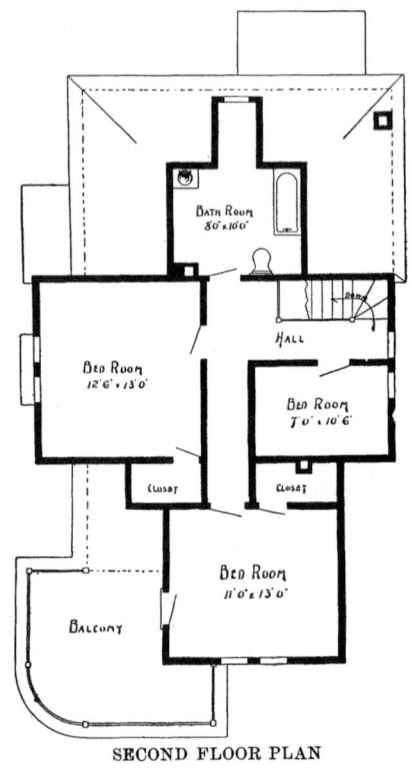

SECOND FLOOR PLAN

Design No. 108
Cost about $1,600

Size: width, 28 feet; length, 43 feet exclusive of porches. Blue prints consist of cellar and foundation plan; first and second floor plans; front, rear, two side elevations; wall sections and all necessary interior details

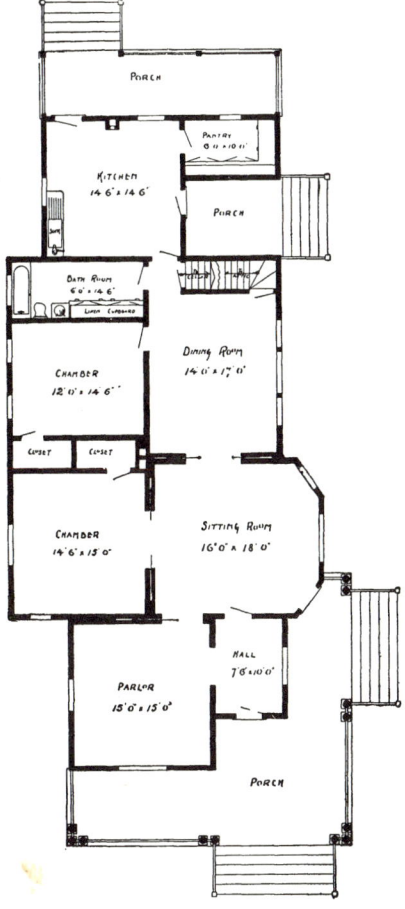

FLOOR PLAN

PRICE of Blue Prints, together with a complete set of typewritten specifications, is

$6.00

Size: width, 34 feet 6 inches; length, 70 feet exclusive of porches. Blue prints consist of cellar and foundation plan; floor plan; front, rear, two side elevations; wall sections and all necessary interior details.

Design No. 77
Cost about $2,000

93

PRICE of Blue Prints, together with a complete set of typewritten specifications, is

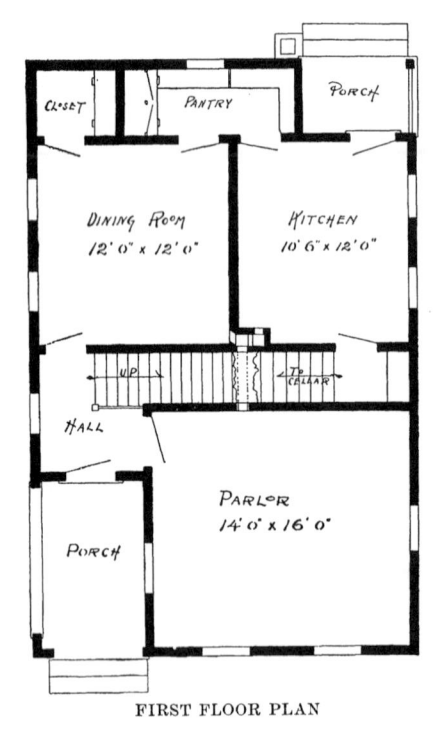

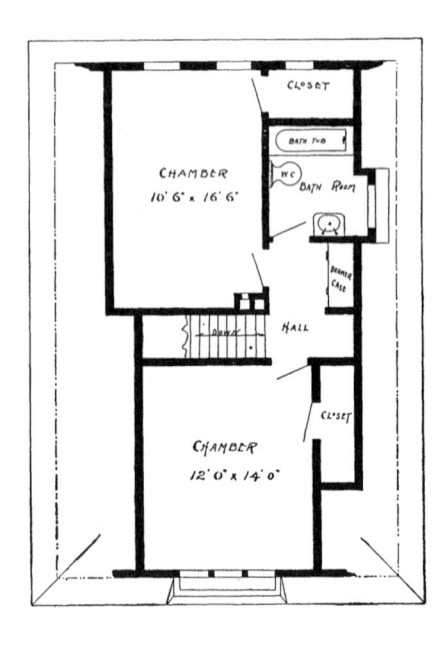

$5.00

FIRST FLOOR PLAN

SECOND FLOOR PLAN

Design No. 92
Cost about $850

Size: width, 24 feet; length, 36 feet. Blue prints consist of cellar and foundation plan; first and second floor plans; front, rear, two side elevations; wall sections and all necessary interior details.

94

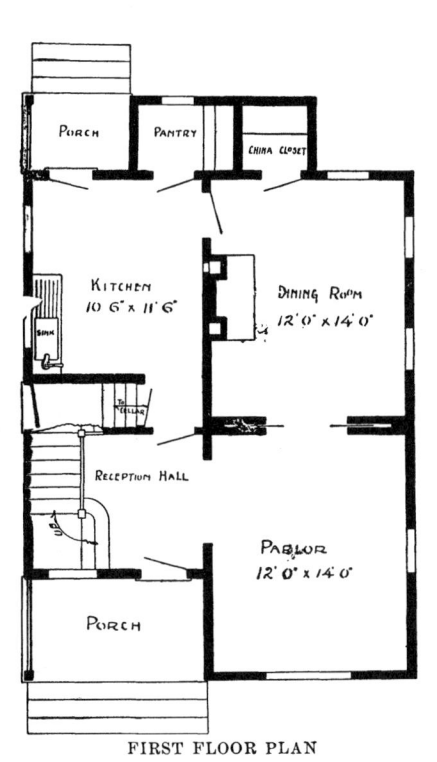

FIRST FLOOR PLAN

SECOND FLOOR PLAN

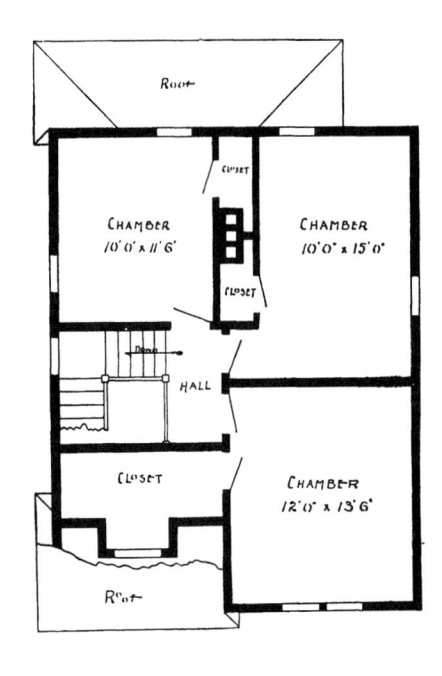

PRICE of Blue Prints, together with a complete set of typewritten specifications, is

$5.00

Size: width, 24 feet; length, 30 feet exclusive of porch. Blue prints consist of cellar and foundation plan; first and second floor plans; front, rear, two side elevations   wall sections and all necessary interior details.

Design No. 66
Cost about $1,350

95

PRICE
of Blue Prints,
together with a
complete set of
typewritten
specifications, is

$12.00

FIRST FLOOR PLAN

SECOND FLOOR PLAN

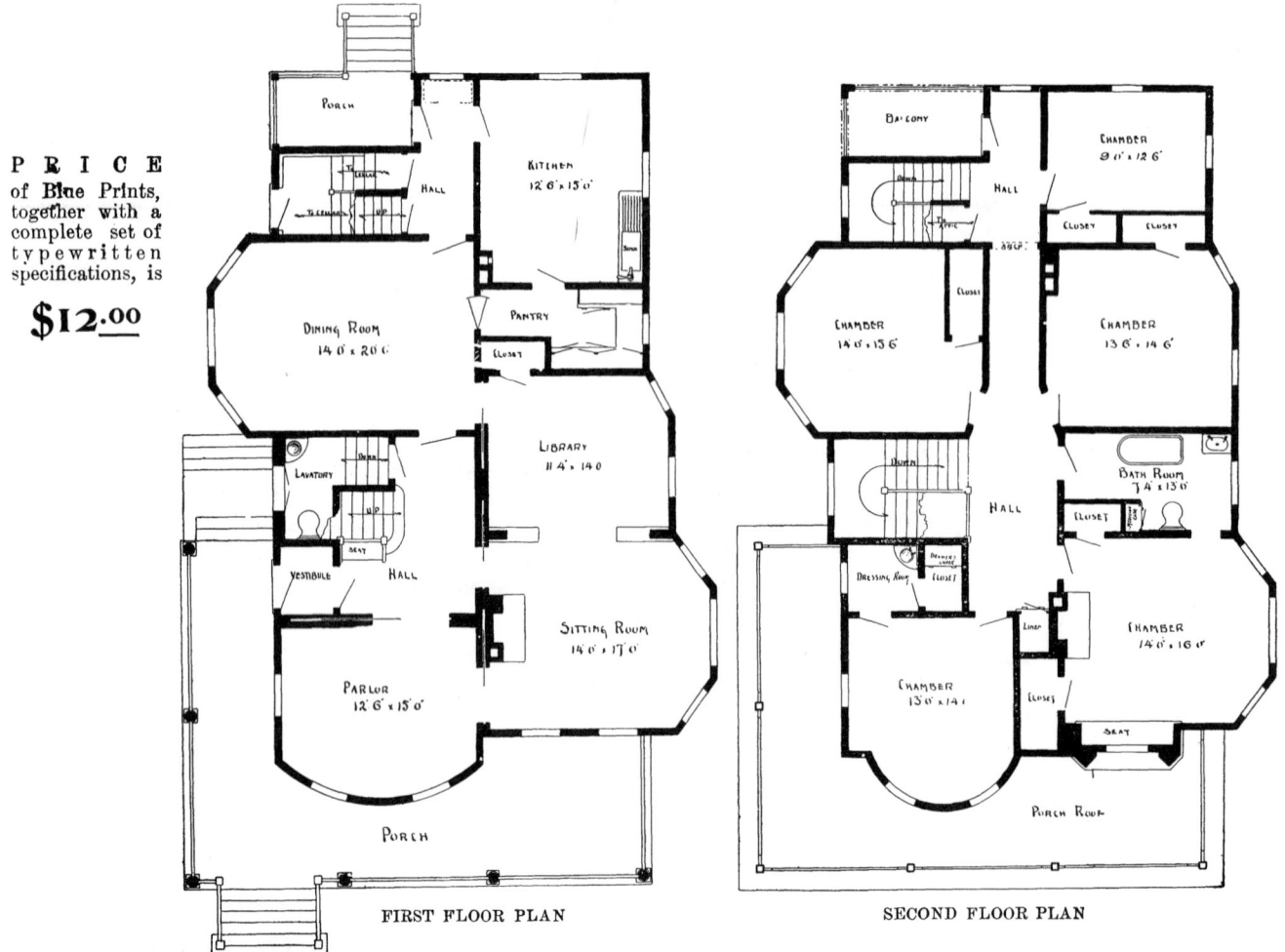

Design No. 60
Cost about $4,000

Size: width, 39 feet; length, 54 feet exclusive of porches. Blue prints consist of cellar and foundation plan; first and second floor plans; attic and roof plan; front, rear, two side elevations; wall sections and all necessary interior details.

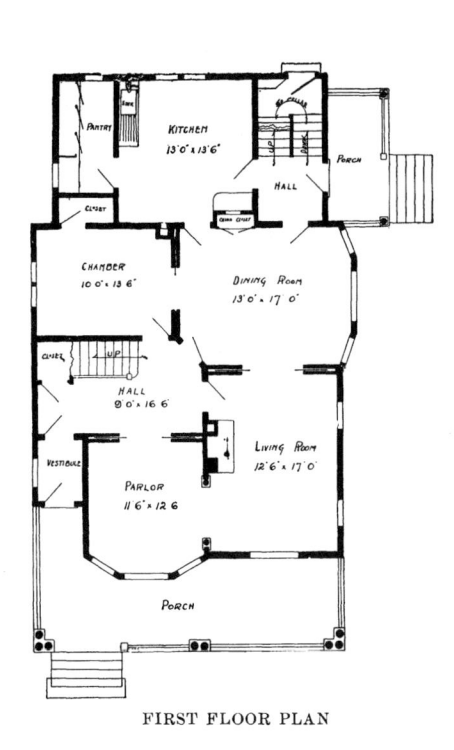

FIRST FLOOR PLAN

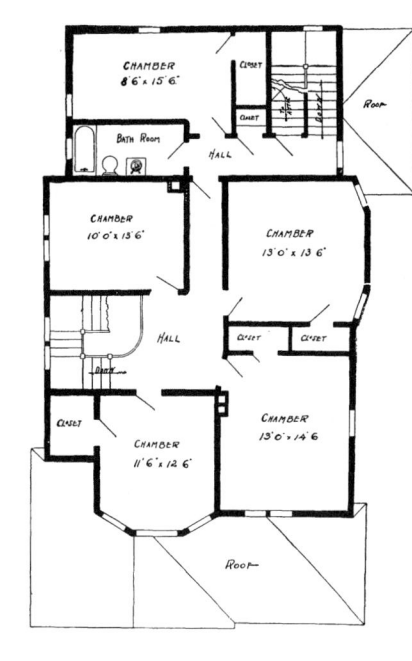

SECOND FLOOR PLAN

PRICE of Blue Prints, together with a complete set of typewritten specifications, is

$8.00

Size: width, 32 feet; length, 48 feet exclusive of porches. Blue prints consist of foundation plan; first and second floor plans; front, rear, two side elevations: wall sections and all necessary interior details.

Design No. 106
Cost about $3,600

PRICE of Blue Prints, together with a complete set of typewritten specifications, is

$5.00

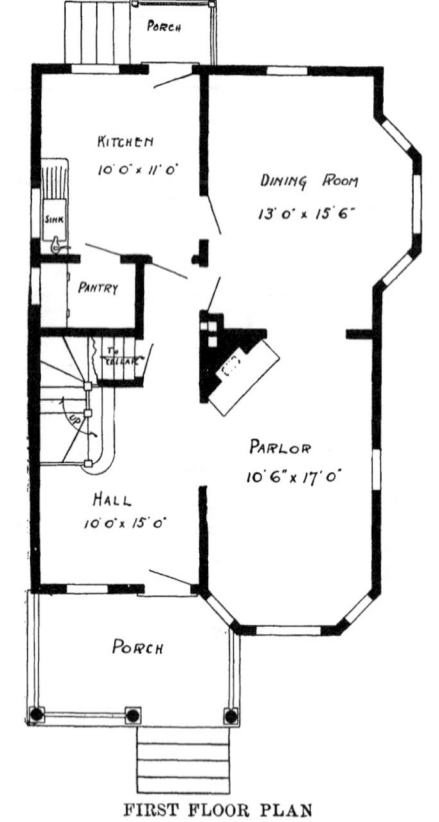

FIRST FLOOR PLAN

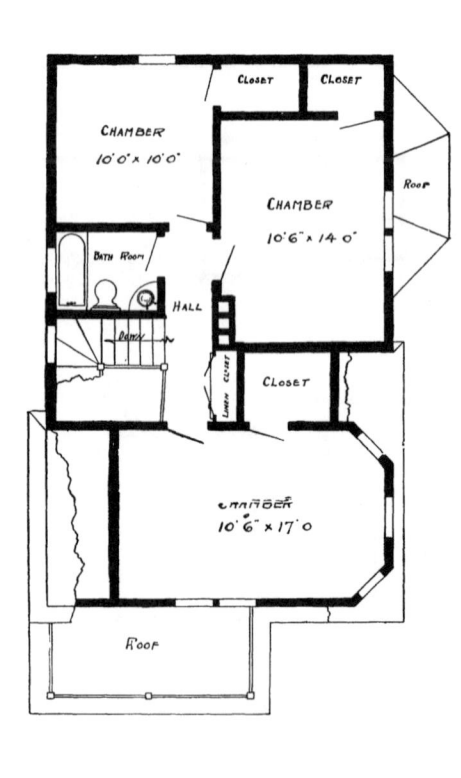

SECOND FLOOR PLAN

Design No. 105
Cost about $1,500

Size: width, 25 feet; length, 34 feet 6 inches exclusive of porches. Blue prints consist of cellar and foundation plan; first and second floor plans; front, rear, two side elevations; wall sections and all necessary interior details.

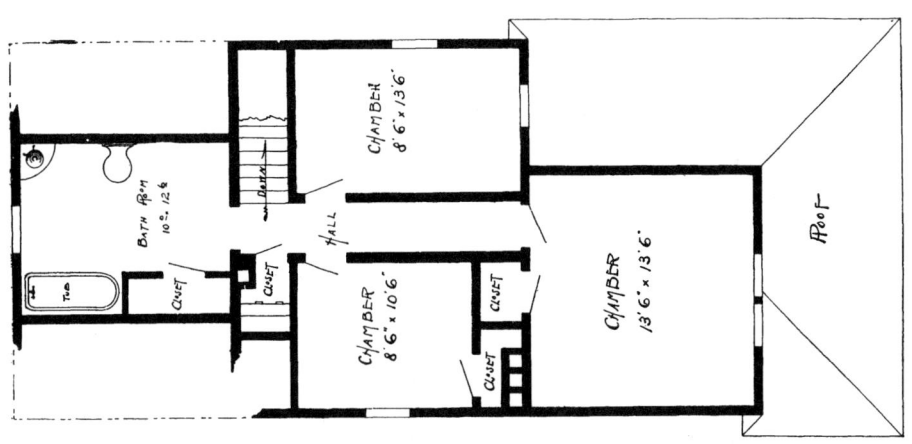

Size: width, 22 feet; length, 45 feet exclusive of porches. Blue prints consist of cellar and foundation plan; first and second floor plans; front, rear, two side elevations; wall sections and all necessary interior details.

PRICE of Blue Prints, together with a complete set of typewritten specifications, is

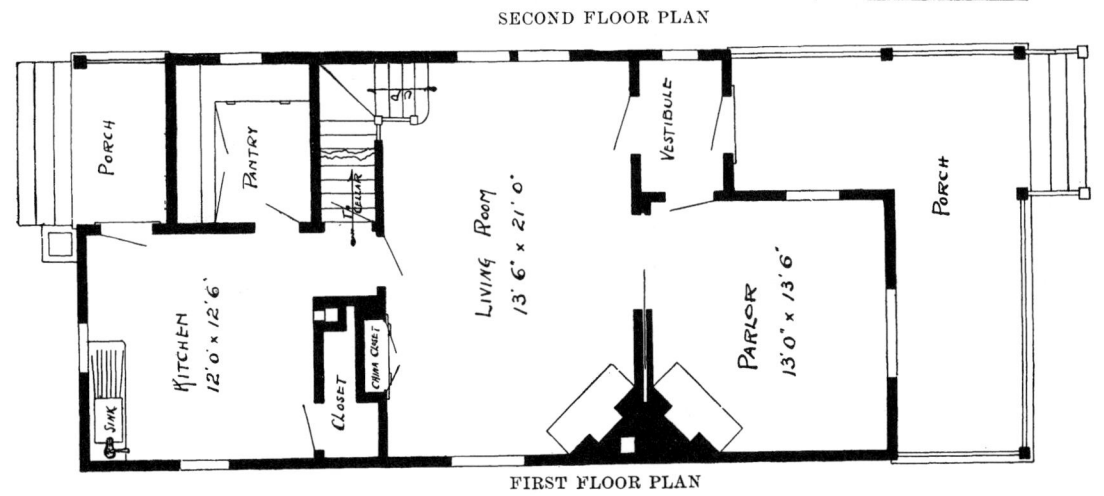

$5.00

Design No. 59
Cost about $1,200

PRICE of Blue Prints, together with a complete set of typewritten specifications, is

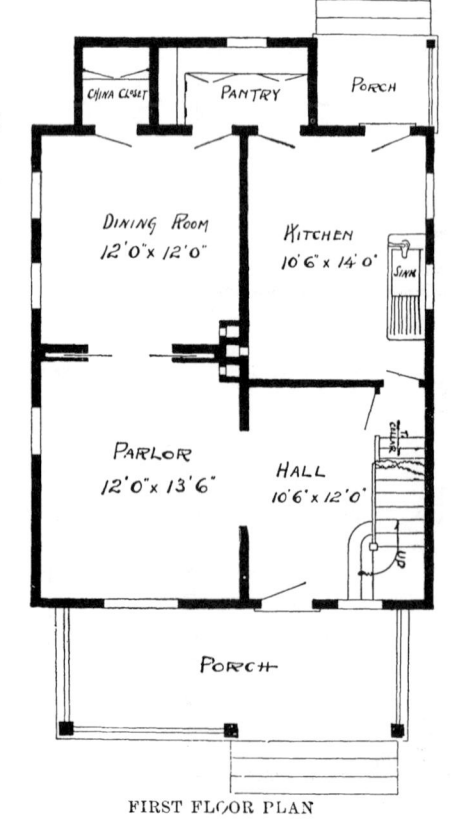

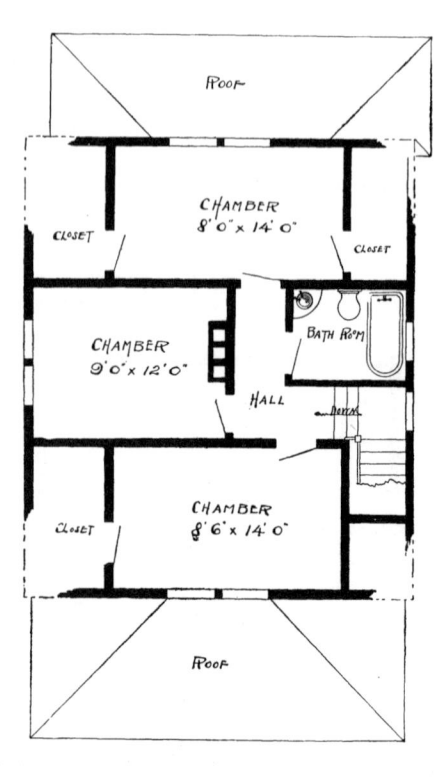

$5.00

FIRST FLOOR PLAN

SECOND FLOOR PLAN

Design No. 13
Cost about $1,000

Size: width, 24 feet; length, 32 feet 6 inches. Blue prints consist of cellar and foundation plan; first and second floor plans; **front, rear, two side** elevations; wall sections and all necessary interior details.

FLOOR PLAN

PRICE of Blue Prints, together with a complete set of typewritten specifications, is

$5.00

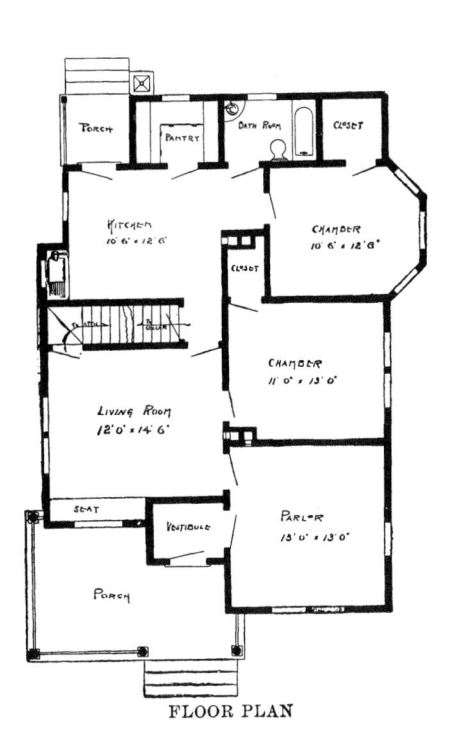

Size: width, 32 feet; length, 42 feet. Blue prints consist of cellar and foundation plan; floor plan; front, rear, two side elevations; wall sections and all necessary interior details.

Design No. 97
Cost about $1,000

101

PRICE of Blue Prints, together with a complete set of typewritten specifications, is

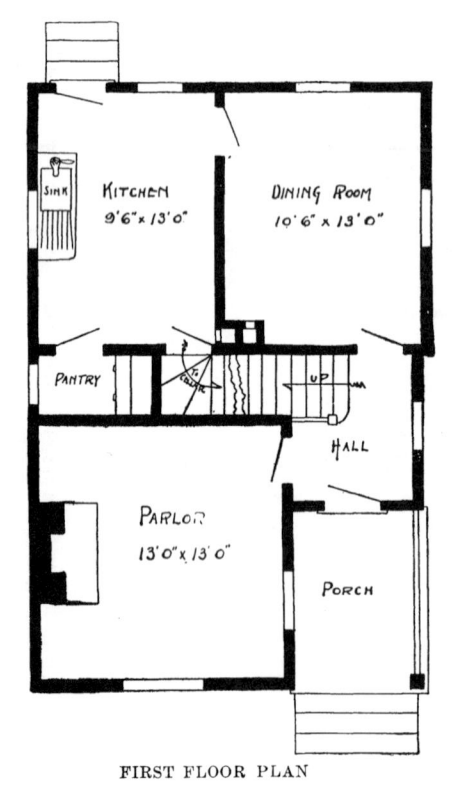

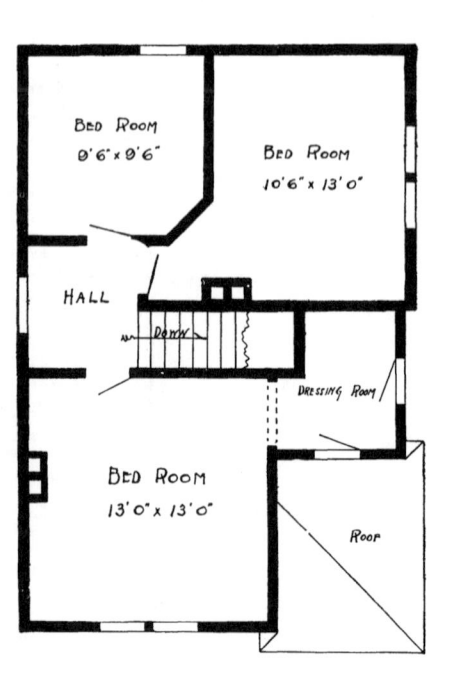

$5.00

FIRST FLOOR PLAN

SECOND FLOOR PLAN

Design No. 103
Cost about $900

Size: width, 20 feet; length, 28 feet exclusive of porches. Blue prints consist of cellar and foundation plan; first and second floor plans; front, rear, two side elevations; wall sections and all necessary interior details.

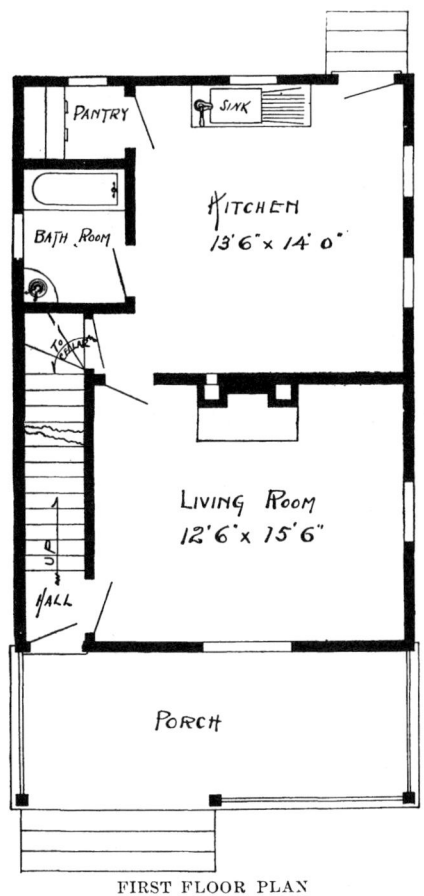

FIRST FLOOR PLAN

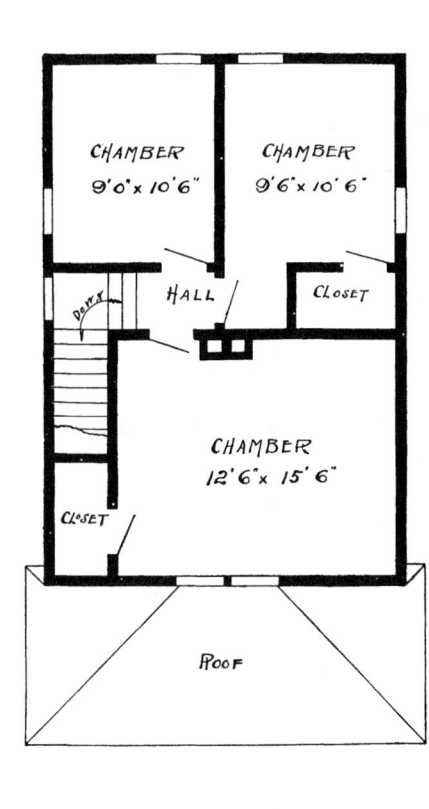

SECOND FLOOR PLAN

PRICE of Blue Prints, together with a complete set of typewritten specifications, is

$5.00

Size: width, 22 feet; length, 31 feet. Blue prints consist of foundation plan; first and second floor plans; front, rear, two side elevations; wall sections and all necessary interior details.

Design No. 104
Cost about $1,150

103

PRICE of Blue Prints, together with a complete set of typewritten specifications, is

$5.00

SECOND FLOOR PLAN

FIRST FLOOR PLAN

Design No. 89
Cost about $1,500

Size: width, 22 feet; length, 38 feet exclusive of porches. Blue prints consist of foundation plan; floor plan; front, rear, two side elevations; wall sections and all necessary interior details.

104

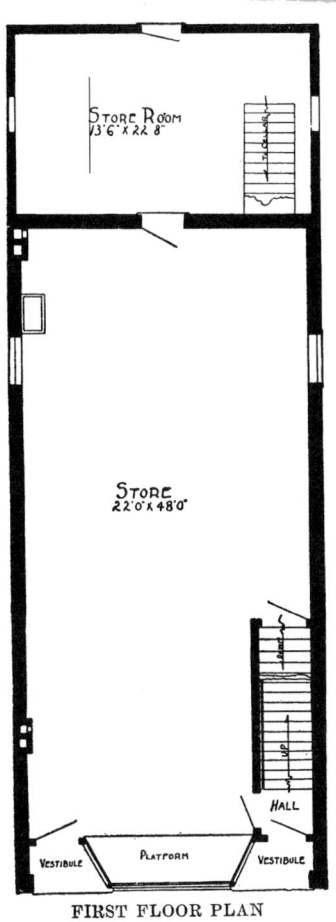

FIRST FLOOR PLAN

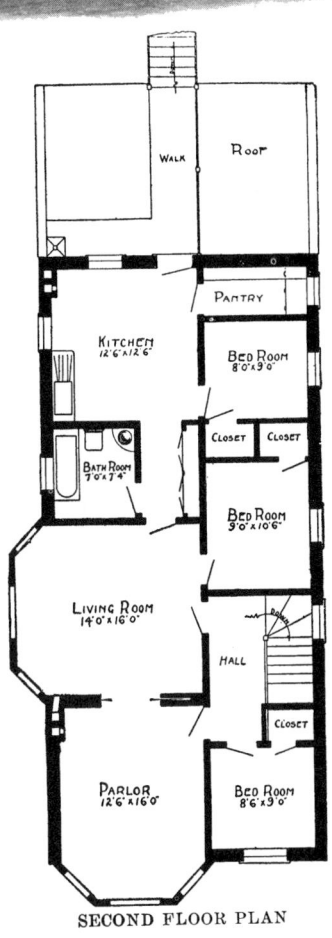

SECOND FLOOR PLAN

PRICE of Blue Prints, together with a complete set of typewritten specifications, is

$10.00

Size: width, 24 feet; length, 64 feet. Blue prints consist of cellar and foundation plan; first and second floor plans; front, rear, two side elevations; wall sections and all necessary interior details.

Design No. 36
Cost about $3,000

105

PRICE
of Blue Prints,
together with a
complete set of
typewritten
specifications, is

$6.00

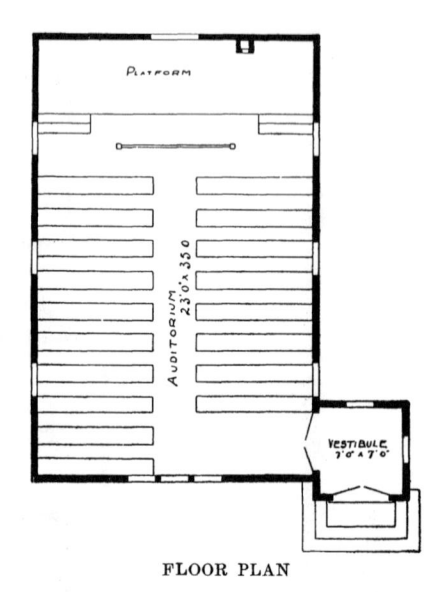

FLOOR PLAN

Design No. 33
Cost about $1,000

Size: width, 24 feet; length, 36 feet exclusive of vestibule. Blue prints consist of foundation plan; floor plan; front, rear, two side elevations; wall sections and all necessary interior details.

FLOOR PLAN

PRICE of Blue Prints, together with a complete set of typewritten specifications, is

$10.00

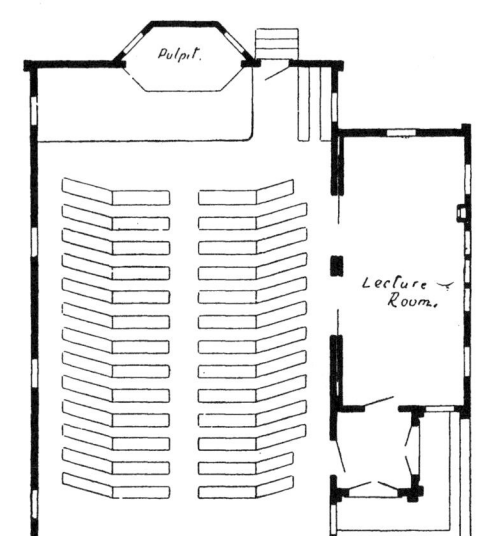

Size: width, 46 feet; length, 50 feet. Blue prints consist of cellar and foundation plan; floor plan; front, rear, two side elevations; wall sections and all necessary interior and exterior details.

Design No. 29
Cost about $2,000

PRICE of Blue Prints, together with a complete set of typewritten specifications, is

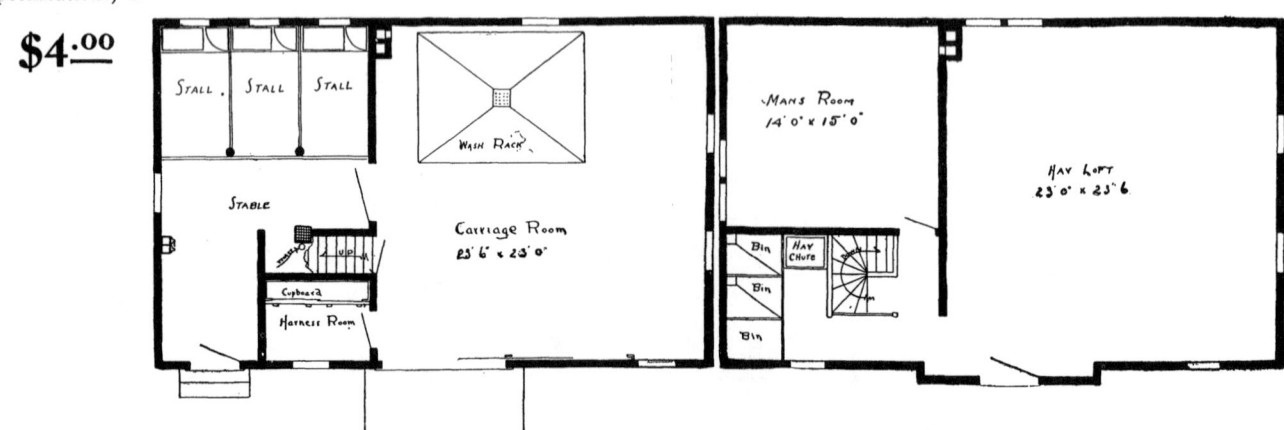

$4.00

FIRST FLOOR PLAN

SECOND FLOOR PLAN

Design No. 28
Cost about $900

Size: width, 40 feet; length, 24 feet. Blue prints consist of foundation plan; first and second floor plans; front, rear, two side elevations and wall sections.

Perspective View Lumber Warehouse Plan No. 31

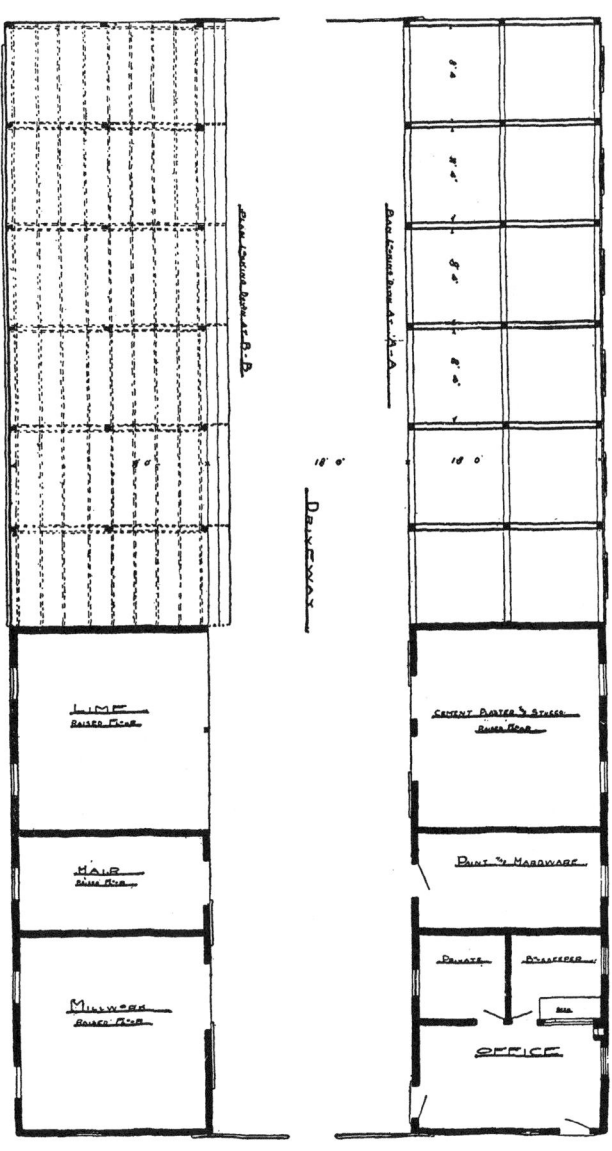

FLOOR PLAN

PRICE of Blue Prints, together with a complete set of typewritten specifications, is

$5.00

Blue prints consist of front elevation, side elevation, floor plans, transverse section and longitudinal section.

INDEX

Design	Page	Cost	Blue Prints	Design	Page	Cost	Blue Prints
1	29	$1,200	$ 4.00	55	82	$550	$4.00
2	28	800	3.00	56	22	4,000	8.00
3	50	650	3.00	57	41	1,500	5.00
4	60	1,000	3.50	58	70	600	3.00
5	31	700	3.00	59	99	1,200	5.00
6	33	1,800	4.00	60	96	4,000	12.00
7	27	6,500	25.00	61	43	750	3.50
8	52	1,350	4.00	62	44	1,600	5.00
9	37	2,500	5.00	63	47	500	3.00
10	34	1,500	4.00	64	48	650	5.00
11	57	2,000	4.50	65	51	575	3.00
12	59	1,700	4.50	66	95	1,350	5.00
13	100	1,000	5.00	67	76	1,000	5.00
14	40	1,500	4.50	68	74	1,550	5.00
15	64	3,700	7.50	69	19	600	5.00
16	39	1,500	5.00	70	77	1,800	6.00
17	13	1,400	5.00	71	8	1,500	5.00
18	58	1,700	4.00	72	25	900	5.00
19	55	1,900	5.00	73	35	2,800	8.00
20	10	850	3.00	74	36	1,000	5.00
21	56	950	3.00	75	30	1,400	5.00
22	23	3,500	12.00	76	18	850	5.00
23	68	2,000	5.00	77	93	2,000	6.00
24	14	900	3.00	78	12	1,000	5.00
25	79	1,900	5.00	79	49	1,500	5.00
26	63	1,800	4.50	80	42	1,700	5.00
27	83	1,500	5.00	81	38	2,000	5.00
28	108	900	4.00	82	5	2,000	5.00
29	107	2,000	10.00	83	45	1,900	5.00
31	109	....	5.00	84	6	1,900	5.00
32	84	600	3.00	85	53	1,400	5.00
33	106	1,000	6.00	86	4	1,500	5.00
34	15	1,100	4.00	87	72	2,700	8.00
35	32	900	4.00	88	75	800	5.00
36	105	3,000	10.00	89	104	1,500	5.00
37	11	1,800	5.00	90	73	800	4.00
38	21	1,000	4.00	91	26	3,000	5.00
39	20	900	4.00	92	94	850	5.00
40	71	2,000	5.00	93	78	1,200	5.00
41	17	2,250	5.00	94	85	2,000	5.00
42	16	500	3.00	95	80	1,250	5.00
43	9	1,750	5.00	96	81	1,250	5.00
44	62	1,600	4.50	97	101	1,000	5.00
45	7	1,300	5.00	98	65	1,800	5.00
46	66	550	3.00	99	86	1,600	5.00
47	67	1,350	4.00	100	87	1,500	5.00
48	24	600	3.00	101	90	2,200	5.00
49	69	1,500	5.00	102	91	1,500	5.00
50	54	650	3.00	103	102	900	5.00
51	46	700	3.00	104	103	1,150	5.00
52	89	2,000	5.00	105	98	1,500	5.00
53	88	2,200	5.00	106	97	3,600	8.00
54	61	2,200	5.00	108	92	1,600	5.00